Lyric Verse

The Odyssey Texts in Types of Literature

Lyric Verse

Edited by **EDWIN RAKOW**

Oak Park and River Forest High School, Oak Park, Illinois

 THE ODYSSEY PRESS · *New York*

Acknowledgments

The editor gratefully acknowledges the kindness of authors, agents, and publishers in giving permission to reproduce material in this anthology, as follows:

ALFRED A. KNOPF, INC.: for "Triad" and "Song" reprinted from *Verse* by Adelaide Crapsey, copyright 1915 by Algernon S. Crapsey, 1934 by Adelaide T. Crapsey. "Dreams" and "Mother to Son" from *The Dream Keeper* by Langston Hughes, copyright 1932 by Langston Hughes. "Golden Bough" from *Collected Poems of Elinor Wylie*, copyright 1932 by Alfred A. Knopf, Inc.

LOUISE ANDREWS: for "I Wish that My Room Had a Floor" from *The Burgess Nonsense Book* by Gelett Burgess.

APPLETON-CENTURY-CROFTS, INC.: for "The Travel Bureau" from: *Narratives in Verse* by Ruth Comfort Mitchell, copyright 1932 by D. Appleton and Company, renewed 1951, reprinted by permission of the publishers Appleton-Century-Crofts, an affiliate of Meredith Press.

BALLANTINE BOOKS, INC.: for "In a Garden" by Donald C. Babcock, reprinted from *New Poems by American Poets*, 1953.

THE BEN ROTH AGENCY, INC.: for "In Flanders Field" by John McCrae © *Punch*. "Jenny Kissed Me" by Paul Dehn, reproduced by permission of *Punch*.

THE BOBBS-MERRILL COMPANY, INC.: for "Sweetes' Li'l' Feller" from *Songs from Dixieland*, by Frank L. Stanton.

BERTON BRALEY: for "To a Photographer," copyright by Berton Braley, all rights reserved.

BRUCE HUMPHRIES, INC.: for "Money" from *Yours for the Asking* by Richard Armour, copyright 1942 by Bruce Humphries, Inc.

CAMBRIDGE UNIVERSITY PRESS: for "Nurse" from *Mountains and Molehills* by Frances Cornford.

CHATTO AND WINDUS LTD.: for "Lone Dog" from *Songs to Save a Soul* by Irene Rutherford McLeod.

THE CLARENDON PRESS: for "All Women Born Are so Perverse" by Robert Bridges.

COWARD-MCCANN, INC.: for "Fragment from Nothing" from *The Creak-*

vi

MCGRAW-HILL BOOK COMPANY, INC.: "Study Habits," "The Love Life (and Death) of a Moose," and "Good Sportsmanship" from *Nights with Armour* by Richard Armour, copyright 1958 by Richard Armour. "To Have and Too Old" and "So Soon" from *Light Armour* by Richard Armour, copyright 1954 by Richard Armour. Used with permission of McGraw-Hill Book Co., Inc.

FAITH B. MAGEE: for "High Flight" from *Sunward I've Climbed* by John G. Magee.

VIRGIL MARKHAM: for "Outwitted" by Edwin Markham.

ELLEN C. MASTERS: for "Mrs. George Reece" from the *Spoon River Anthology* by Edgar Lee Masters, published by The Macmillan Company.

FLORENCE RIPLEY MASTIN AND THE NEW YORK TIMES: for "Eight-Cylinder Man."

HUGHES MEARNS: for "The Little Man Who Wasn't There" and "The Perfect Reactionary."

METHUEN & CO. LTD.: for "The Welsh" by E. V. Lucas.

NEW DIRECTIONS: for "Dawn" from *The Collected Earlier Poems of William Carlos Williams*, copyright 1938, 1951 by William Carlos Williams. Reprinted by permission of New Directions, publishers.

THE NEW YORKER: for "Tele-News Blues" by Peter Dufault, © 1952 The New Yorker Magazine, Inc. "I Sometimes Think" by E. P. Lister, © 1959 The New Yorker Magazine, Inc.

OXFORD UNIVERSITY PRESS: for "A Kiss" from *The Poetical Works of Austin Dobson*.

PAUL ELDER & COMPANY: for "Be Strong" by Maltbie Davenport Babcock.

THE REILLY & LEE COMPANY: for "All that Matters" from *All that Matters* by Edgar A. Guest, copyright the Reilly & Lee Company, Chicago.

ALMA J. SARETT: for "Four Little Foxes" from *Covenant with Earth* by Lew Sarett, edited and copyrighted, 1956, by Alma Johnson Sarett, Gainesville: University of Florida Press, 1956.

CHARLES SCRIBNER'S SONS: The following poems are reprinted with the permission of Charles Scribner's Sons: "Four Things" from *The Builders* (1897) by Henry van Dyke and "I Have a Rendezvous with Death" from *Poems* by Alan Seeger, copyright 1916 Charles Scribner's Sons, renewal copyright 1944 Elsie Adams Seeger.

THE SEWANEE REVIEW AND EUGENE M. KAYDEN: for "Manhattan Skyline" by Eugene M. Kayden.

SIMON AND SCHUSTER, INC.: for selections from *A Space Child's Mother Goose* © 1958 by Frederick Winson and Marion Parry.

THE SOCIETY OF AUTHORS: for "Infant Innocence" by A. E. Housman and "The Fly" by Walter de la Mare, permission granted by The

To the Teachers Who Will Use This Book

LYRIC VERSE has been planned as a companion volume to Max T. Hohn's *Stories in Verse*. Like that text, *Lyric Verse* is designed to persuade doubting young people that poetry can become a joyous and meaningful part of their lives.

In this text the word *lyric* is used in its broadest sense. It includes didactic, descriptive, satiric—all types of poetry other than narrative with the exception of drama in verse. The selections range from the song to the ode, from the flippancy of light verse to the dignity of the reflective lyric, from the simple ditty to the more complex French forms.

Lyric Verse, like all *The Odyssey Texts in Types of Literature*, is a textbook meant to be used by a teacher in a class situation. The teacher *teaches*; the student *learns*. The book is edited on the assumption that the average student will more readily learn from a clearly stated purpose and objective than from a situation in which he is expected somehow to absorb vague aspects and values of poetry by a process of osmosis.

Part One aims to give the student insight into the sources of pleasure offered by the lyric as a type and a knowledge of the craftsmanship which contributes to a poem's overall effectiveness. (Some technical terms of prosody are defined in footnotes, so they will be available for those students who can profit by knowing them.) Having acquired this knowledge, the student is ready to apply it to the extensive reading in Part Two.

Part One opens with a section devoted to light verse—poems for fun. These poems serve as an appetizer, and they also make young readers aware of the sheer delight that lyric verse has to offer. The student is, moreover, introduced to the fact that fun in a particular poem may have a barb in it—satire. The forms of some of these poems, such as the limerick and the triolet, can easily be imitated by the student.

The next section of Part One explains the emotional characteristics of the lyric. The student learns that we all need an outlet for our emotions and that writing lyric poetry can serve as such. He discovers that he has on occasion found release for his emotions by being something of a lyric poet himself. He also discovers that, since poets are probably more skillful than he at expressing their emotions in words, he can find release for his emotions by reading and memorizing the poems of others. Lastly, the student learns that by reading lyric poetry he can vicariously extend his emotional experiences and thus grow emotionally.

The third section introduces the student to the pleasures of music-in-words. Here he gains understanding of how the music of poetry helps to express the full meaning and emotion in the mind and heart of the poet. He learns some of the elementary techniques of the poet's craft. This section concludes with a simple presentation of a few of the common stanzaic patterns; the use of blank verse in the lyric; and the sonnet as a poetic form. (The spelling *rime* instead of *rhyme* is used throughout this text because it is useful in eradicating the students' confusion between *rhyme* and *rhythm*.)

The fourth section further analyzes the poet's craft. This section is the most difficult in the text. It includes a discussion of imagery and its sensuous delights. It presents four common figures of speech (simile, metaphor, personification, symbol), each illustrated by a complete poem. A particular effort has been made to clarify the difficult concept of the symbol.

The fifth and last section of Part One is concerned with the inspirational function of poetry. The student should come to see how in a lyric poem thought, emotion, music, and imagery all combine to create a meaningful experience, one with a bit of glory in it.

Part Two is a little anthology of lyric verse. Each poem has been selected on its merit and for its student appeal. The arrangement is roughly from the easy to the more complex. In the way of editorial helps, most of the poems are introduced with headnotes, which guide the student to seek particulars.

Some poems have marginal aids designed to help the student get the meaning. The endnotes consist of questions or suggestions to insure rich class discussion.

Really good oral reading of lyric verse is worthy of much emphasis. It not only trains readers how to bring the poetry alive but also makes intelligent and appreciative listeners. Only by reading aloud can the student deeply feel the emotional impact of a particular lyric. Only by hearing a poem read aloud will the student become sensitive to the manifold rhythms that verse is full of.

To my friends and students who have shared in the making of this book, I express appreciation. To the late Max T. Hohn, through his *Stories in Verse*, I am greatly indebted. I want especially to thank James Berkley, Perry Congdon, and Donald Rehkopf, my colleagues at Oak Park and River Forest High School, for their valuable suggestions and criticisms; and a very warm regard and gratitude to John Gehlmann, who is really co-editor of this book.

E. R.

Contents

PART ONE

Sources of Pleasure in Lyric Verse

PART TWO

More Lyric Verse to Read for Enjoyment

Lyric Verse

To the Students Who Will Use This Book

POETRY is usually divided into three main groups: narrative, dramatic, and lyric. You are probably already familiar with narrative and dramatic poetry; this book introduces you to the third type—lyric verse.

A lyric poem is a melodic and imaginative expression of the author's personal thoughts and feelings about some subject. The thought and emotion expressed may be either simple or complex; lyric verse records both the great utterances of noble hearts and the melodic wit of playful minds.

All of us react in mind and heart to objects, situations, and events. We think, we meditate, we worry, we toy with ideas, we say we philosophize (often without quite knowing what that means). We get irked or embarrassed; we get silly with joy or silent with sorrow. If you have ever tried to express your feelings or thoughts in musical and moving language, you have been an amateur in lyric verse.

In this book the term *lyric* is used to cover a number of different kinds of poems: those which instruct (didactic), or describe (descriptive), or ridicule (satiric), as well as those which sing. In fact, all sorts of poems that do *not* tell a story are included.

Lyric Verse consists of two parts. Part One tells you the sources of pleasure to be found in lyric verse. Part Two is an anthology of lyric poems. In reading Part Two you should apply the knowledge gained from your study of Part One. You will, I hope, find these poems amusing, melodic, moving, and inspiring. I very much hope that through the study of *Lyric Verse* you will come not only to enjoy poems of this type but also to feel deeply that there is something of real fiber to a lyric poem in addition to

1

mere rime and pretty words, however enjoyable these can be in themselves.

Perhaps in this book you will find "some bit of verse of truth or beauty" that will "serve a turn in your life," as a line from Alexander Pope's poetry served Mrs. George Reece. Here is her story as she tells it in Edgar Lee Masters' *Spoon River Anthology:*

MRS. GEORGE REECE

To this generation I would say:
Memorize some bit of verse of truth or beauty.
It may serve a turn in your life.
My husband had nothing to do
With the fall of the bank—he was only cashier.   5
The wreck was due to the president, Thomas Rhodes,
And his vain, unscrupulous son.
Yet my husband was sent to prison,
And I was left with the children,
To feed and clothe and school them.   10
And I did it, and sent them forth
Into the world all clean and strong,
And all through the wisdom of Pope, the poet:
"Act well your part, there all the honor lies."

Through the poems and editorial aids in this book, I want you to become not merely fulfillers of a day's assignment but life readers of poems—poems in newspapers, in magazines, in anthologies, in volumes of verse.

And I must insist: poetry must be read aloud. To read a poem silently is as absurd as to take a sheet of music and read it through silently. A poem, like a song, is intended to be performed orally by someone. It is too bad that you and I cannot be born superb oral readers of poems. Then we would surely move others and be moved. We could make the reading of and listening to poetry as fascinating and as haunting as the drum beat in the jungle. Fortunately we can learn—by practice.

PART ONE

Sources of Pleasure in Lyric Verse

Lyric Laughter

LYRIC VERSE gives you pleasure through its varied wit and humor, producing smiles, laughs, chortles, or guffaws, as the poets range from the witty, droll, comic, to the ludicrous and the ridiculous.

I open *Lyric Verse* with a short sampling of humorous lyrics to remind you of the fun you can find in this type of literature and also to whet your appetite with an *hors d'oeuvre* before the major courses of the feast, which are presented in the succeeding sections.

Nothing is more varied and personal than taste in humor. A poem which amuses one person may to another seem dull, or stupid, or crude, or even immoral. *De gustibus non est disputandum* ("There can be no argument in matters of taste") applies in this category as in few others. However, most cultivated persons include among their favorites the witty and the satirical, poems in which the writer looks below the surface and makes some incisive comment on life.

In this opening section I have gathered together examples of as wide a variety of humorous verse as space permits. Included are bits of nonsense, macabre verse, limericks, triolets. I hope some of them will make you chuckle and will ease for a moment the tensions of the day.

Society Verse

Let us start with some bits of "society verse" * which I personally consider especially amusing.

* *Society verse* (*vers de société*) is brief lyrical verse written in a graceful, polished, crisp, sparkling, playful mood.

GOOD SPORTSMANSHIP
Richard Armour

Good sportsmanship we hail, we sing,
  It's always pleasant when you spot it.
There's only one unhappy thing:
  You have to lose to prove you've got it.

STUDY HABITS
Richard Armour

Peanut butter thickly spread
On crispy crackers and on bread,
Potato-chips and chunks of cheese,
Chocolates and cake—it's these
With which our teen-age daughter crams   5
For exams.

TO HAVE AND TOO OLD
Richard Armour

The bride, white of hair, is stooped over her cane,
  Her faltering footsteps need guiding,
While down the church aisle, with a wan, toothless smile,
  The groom in a wheel chair comes riding.

And who is this elderly couple, you ask?   5
  You'll find, when you've closely explored it,
That here is that rare, most conservative pair,
  Who waited till they could afford it.

SO SOON?
Richard Armour

Our guests are about to go—
The signs, it is true, are small,

6

But the sensitive host and hostess
Know they'll soon be out in the hall.

Our guests are about to go—   5
That is, they're all set to start
To plan to prepare to get ready
To begin to commence to depart.

THE LOVE LIFE (AND DEATH) OF A MOOSE
Richard Armour

(Up in Newfoundland some 30 moose, mistaking Diesel train horns
for mating calls, have been lured to death on the tracks. *News item*.)

Imagine this beast of the frozen Northeast
With its annual amorous craze on,
Seduced by the toot of a choo-choo en route
Into making a fatal liaison.

Conceive of its sighs as it straddles the ties,   5
Unaware of the killer it's dating.
The honk of the train has gone straight to its brain,
And its mind is completely on mating.

Appalling? Of course, but just think how much worse
It would be, and no words shall we weasel,   10
Should an engine tear loose from its tracks when a moose
Makes what sounds like the call of a Diesel.

THE NAUGHTY PREPOSITION
Morris Bishop

I lately lost a preposition;
   It hid, I thought, beneath my chair.
And angrily I cried: "Perdition!
   Up from out of in under there!"

Correctness is my *vade mecum,*   5
   And straggling phrases I abhor;
And yet I wondered: "What should he come
   Up from out of in under for?"

5. *Vade mecum (va de mé kum)*: Constant companion. The phrase is
Latin for "go with me."

MARBLE-TOP

E. B. White

At counters where I eat my lunch
   In dim arcades of industry,
I cock my elbows up and munch
   Whatever food occurs to me.

By many mirrors multiplied   5
   My silly face is not exalted;
And when I leave I have inside
   An egg-and-lettuce and a malted.

And just to hear the pretty peal
   Of merry maids at their pimento   10
Is more to me than any meal
   Or banquet that I ever went to.

THE WELSH

E. V. Lucas

If you enjoy Welsh rabbits, this little lyric will amuse you.
And never call it a "Welsh rarebit" again!

The gallant Welsh, of all degrees,
Have one delightful habit;
They cover toast with melted cheese,
And call the thing a rabbit.
And though no fur upon it grows,   5

And though it has no twitching nose,
Nor twinkling tail behind it,
As reputable rabbits should;
Yet taste a piece, and very good,
I'm bound to say, you'll find it.   10

THE PERFECT HUSBAND
Ogden Nash

Ogden Nash has made a special place for himself in the field of humorous poetry. His specialties are a certain irregular prose-poetry rhythm and an original conception of the kinds of words and line lengths that can be made to rime with each other.

He tells you when you've got on too much lipstick,
And helps you with your girdle when your hips stick.

CELERY
Ogden Nash

Celery, raw,
Develops the jaw,
But celery, stewed,
Is more quietly chewed.

THIS IS GOING TO HURT JUST A LITTLE BIT
Ogden Nash

One thing I like less than most things is sitting in a dentist chair
    with my mouth wide open,
And that I will never have to do it again is a hope that I am
    against hope hopen.
Because some tortures are physical and some are mental,
But the one that is both is dental.

It is hard to be self-possessed
With your jaw digging into your chest,
So hard to retain your calm
When your fingernails are making serious alterations in your life
    line or love line or some other important line in your palm;
So hard to give your usual effect of cheery benignity
When you know your position is one of the two or three in life
    most lacking in dignity.   10
And your mouth is like a section of road that is being worked on,
And it is all cluttered up with stone crushers and concrete mixers
    and drills and steam rollers and there isn't a nerve of your
    head that you aren't being irked on.
Oh, some people are unfortunate enough to be strung up by
    thumbs,
And others have things done to their gums,
And your teeth are supposed to be being polished,   15
But you have reason to believe they are being demolished,
And the circumstance that adds most to your terror
Is that it's all being done with a mirror,
Because the dentist may be a bear, or as the Romans used to say,
    only they were referring to a feminine bear when they said
    it, an *ursa*,
But all the same how can you be sure when he takes his crowbar
    in one hand and mirror in the other, he won't get mixed up,
    the way you do when you try to tie a bow tie with the aid
    of a mirror, and forget that left is right and *vice versa?*   20
And then at last he says That will be all; but it isn't because he
    then coats your mouth from cellar to roof
With something that I suspect is generally used to put a shine on
    a horse's hoof,
And you totter to your feet and think, Well it's all over now
    and after all it was only this once,
And he says come back in three monce.
And this, O Fate, is the most vicious circle that thou ever
    sentest,   25
That Man has to go continually to the dentist to keep his teeth in
    good condition when the chief reason he wants his teeth in
    good condition is so that he won't have to go to the dentist.

Among all the foregoing poems which did you find amusing? Which ones left you "cold"? Can you suggest any reasons for your choices? Perhaps there are none; you may wish to quote Thomas Browne's famous quatrain:

> I do not love thee, Doctor Fell,
> The reason why I cannot tell;
> But this alone I know full well,
> I do not love thee, Doctor Fell.

You will find more entertainment in the collected poems of the authors who amused you. And a few other names and titles have been included in the following list.

Richard Armour
LIGHT ARMOUR
NIGHTS WITH ARMOUR

Morris Bishop
BOWL OF BISHOP

Samuel Hoffenstein
POEMS IN PRAISE OF PRACTICALLY NOTHING
YEAR IN YOU'RE OUT

Felicia Lamport
SCRAP IRONY

E. V. Lucas
PLAYTIME & COMPANY

Phyllis McGinley
POCKETFUL OF WRY
TIMES THREE
LOVE LETTERS OF PHYLLIS MCGINLEY

Ogden Nash
FAMILY REUNION
PARENTS KEEP OUT
SELECTED VERSES
VERSES FROM 1929 ON

Dorothy Parker
COLLECTED POETRY

E. B. White
THE LADY IS COLD AND OTHER POEMS

Limericks

One of the commonest forms of humorous verse is the five-line poem known as the limerick. I am sure you have heard many limericks and have some favorites. Here are a few in which I have found special delight.

There was a young lady named Bright,
Who traveled much faster than light.
   She started one day
   In the relative way,
And returned on the previous night.
Anonymous

There was an old man of Antigua,
Whose wife said, "My dear, what a pig you are!"
   He replied, "O my queen,
   Is it manners you mean,
Or do you refer to my fig-u-a?"
Anonymous

There was a young lady from Del.
Who was most undoubtedly wel.
   That to dress for a masque
   Wasn't much of a tasque,
But she cried, "What the heck will my fel.?"
Anonymous

There was an enchanting young bride
But from eating green apples she died.
   They soon had fermented
   Within the lamented
And made cider inside her inside.
Anonymous

There was a young man from Japan
Whose limericks never would scan;
    When they said it was so,
    He replied, "Yes, I know,
But I always try to get as many words into the last line as ever I
    possibly can."

Anonymous

Although the origin of the limerick is shrouded in obscurity, the
following has often been credited—falsely—as the first.

    There was a young lady of Niger
    Who smiled as she rode on a tiger.
        They returned from the ride
        With the lady inside
    And the smile on the face of the tiger.

The limerick is probably the easiest verse form to follow. In writing
your own limerick, be sure to make the last line a good one. Perhaps
your teacher will stage for you a limerick contest and have a class vote
decide which ones are the best. Or the teacher may write the first four
lines of a limerick, submit these to the class, and offer a prize for the
best fifth line.

Parodies

A parody is an imitation, for comic effect, of the style and con-
tent of some piece of literature. Of course, the humor depends
upon the reader's knowledge of the original.

To illustrate parodies for you, I submit a well-known little
poem by Leigh Hunt and two parodies of it.

JENNY KISS'D ME
Leigh Hunt

Jenny kiss'd me when we met,
    Jumping from the chair she sat in;
Time, you thief, who love to get
    Sweets into your list, put that in!

13

Say I'm weary, say I'm sad, 5
   Say that health and wealth have miss'd me,
Say I'm growing old, but add,
   Jenny kiss'd me.

"JENNY KISS'D ME WHEN WE MET"
Paul Dehn

Jenny kiss'd me when we met,
   Jumping from the chair she sat in;
Time, you thief, who love to get
   Sweets into your list, put that in!
Say I'm weary, say I'm old, 5
   Say that health and wealth have miss'd me,
Say I've had a filthy cold
   Since Jenny kiss'd me.

"SUCH STUFF AS DREAMS"
Franklin P. Adams

Jenny kiss'd me in a dream;
   So did Elsie, Lucy, Cora,
Bessie, Gwendolyn, Eupheme,
   Alice, Adelaide, and Dora.
Say of honor I'm devoid, 5
   Say monogamy has miss'd me,
But don't say to Dr. Freud
   Jenny kiss'd me.

Which of these three poems did you find most amusing, the original or one of the parodies?

What is the natural reaction to a parody of a poem which one loves in the original?

Try to find a copy of either Louis Untermeyer's *Collected Parodies* or Carolyn Wells's *Parody Anthology* and read other amusing parodies.

Triolets

Among the various French forms of light verse perhaps the best known is the triolet.

THE KISS
Austin Dobson

Rose kissed me today—
Will she kiss me tomorrow?
Let it be as it may,
Rose kissed me *today;*
But the pleasure gives way   5
To a savor of sorrow;
Rose kissed me today—
Will she kiss me tomorrow?

TRIOLET
William Ernest Henley

Easy is the triolet
  If you really learn to make it!
Once a neat refrain you get,
Easy is the triolet.
As you see!—I pay my debt   5
  With another rhyme. Deuce take it,
Easy is the triolet,
  If you really learn to make it!

TRIOLET AGAINST SISTERS
Phyllis McGinley

Sisters are always drying their hair.
  Locked into rooms, alone,

They pose at the mirror, shoulders bare,
Trying this way and that their hair,
Or fly importunate down the stair   5
    To answer the telephone.
Sisters are always drying their hair,
    Locked into rooms, alone.

TRIOLET

Robert Bridges

All women born are so perverse,
    No man need boast their love possessing,
If nought seems better, nothing's worse;
All women born are so perverse,
From Adam's wife that proved a curse   5
    Though God had made her for a blessing.
All women born are so perverse,
    No man need boast their love possessing.

The triolet is a poem of eight lines, with lines 1 and 2 repeated as 7 and 8. Line 4 is also line 1 repeated. Lines 3 and 5 rime with line 1, and line 6 rimes with line 2.

If you wish to try your hand at a triolet, you will discover that having written lines 1 and 2, you have already completed five of the eight lines of the poem:

1.	Of all the newer dances	A
2.	I like the cha-cha best	B
3.		a
4.	Of all the newer dances	A
5.		a
6.		b
7.	Of all the newer dances	A
8.	I like the cha-cha best.	B

Now all you need to do is to compose two lines riming with *dances* and one line riming with *best*. You must be careful to make lines 3, 4, 5, and 6 read smoothly.

Satire

Satire is a branch of literature which endeavors to improve human institutions by ridiculing vice or folly. It may be gentle and smiling or bitter and angry.

Here are three bits of satire of the gentler sort. The first pokes fun at the omnipresent sets of perfect teeth on television programs; the second, at our national political conventions; the third, at those who (we hope not too seriously) have found life not worth living and threaten "to end it all."

REFLECTIONS DENTAL
Phyllis McGinley

How pure, how beautiful, how fine
Do teeth on television shine!
No flutist flutes, no dancer twirls,
But comes equipped with matching pearls.
Gleeful announcers all are born   5
With sets like rows of hybrid corn.
Clowns, critics, clergy, commentators,
Ventriloquists and roller skaters,
M.C.s who beat their palms together,
The girl who diagrams the weather,   10
The crooner crooning for his supper—
All flash white treasures, lower and upper.
With miles of smiles the airwaves teem,
And each an orthodontist's dream.

'Twould please my eye as gold a miser's—   15
One charmer with uncapped incisors.

What words or phrases made you chuckle?

GREATEST SHOW ON EARTH
The National Convention
Felicia Lamport

See the scrimmage and the scrabble
Hear the raucous rabble's babble
   And the ribald rebels' ricocheting roar
While the Chairman pounds his gavel
Trying vainly to unravel   5
All the barking carking cavil
   On the floor.

Strange, the leaders seem untroubled
Though the hubbub has redoubled
   And the level of the revel is a blast,   10
For the mission, by tradition,
Of the party politician
Is to foster fuss and fission
   To the last.

When at last The Man is chosen   15
What togetherness then flows in!
   Every enemy becomes a bosom friend.
See the opposition buckle,
Watch the truculent ones truckle;
Under, every man will knuckle   20
   At the end.

What details of our political convention and system are satirized?
Why is "togetherness" in the last stanza a word of ridicule?

RÉSUMÉ
Dorothy Parker

Razors pain you;
Rivers are damp;

Acids stain you;
And drugs cause cramp.
Guns aren't lawful;   5
Nooses give;
Gas smells awful;
You might as well live.

(For more satirical poems see pp. 196, 200, and 202.)

Macabre Humor

The squeamish student should skip this section. It is only for misguided souls, like your editor, who wilfully enjoy the gruesome.

PATIENCE
Harry Graham

When ski-ing in the Engadine
My hat blew off down a ravine.
My son, who went to fetch it back,
Slipped through an icy glacier's crack
And then got permanently stuck.   5
It really was infernal luck:
My hat was practically new—
I loved my little Henry too—
And I may have to wait for years
Till either of them reappears.   10

AUNT ELIZA
Harry Graham

In the drinking-well
    Which the plumber built her,
Aunt Eliza fell. . . .
    . . . We must buy a filter.

EGOISM

W. Craddle

I am anxious after praise;
I sometimes wish it were not so:
I hate to think I spend my days
Waiting for what I'll never know.

I even hope that when I'm dead   5
The worms won't find me wholly vicious,
But, as they masticate my head,
Will smack their lips and cry, "Delicious!"

INFANT INNOCENCE

A. E. Housman

The Grizzly Bear is huge and wild;
He has devoured the infant child.
The infant child is not aware
He has been eaten by the bear.

Nonsense

And now for a bit of nonsense—absurd, foolish, preposterous.
I hope you agree that
"A little nonsense now and then
Is relished by the best of men."

'TIS MIDNIGHT

Anonymous

'Tis midnight, and the setting sun
Is slowly rising in the west;
The rapid rivers slowly run,
The frog is on his downy nest.

20

The pensive goat and sportive cow,   5
Hilarious, leap from bough to bough.

I WISH THAT MY ROOM HAD A FLOOR
Gelett Burgess

I wish that my room had a floor;
I don't care so much for a door,
But this walking around
Without touching the ground
Is getting to be such a bore!

"THE SPACE CHILD'S MOTHER GOOSE"
Three Rimes
Frederick Winsor

10

This little pig built a spaceship,
This little pig paid the bill;
This little pig made isotopes,
This little pig ate a pill;
And this little pig did nothing at all,   5
But he's just a little pig still.

17

Little Jack Horner
Sits in a corner
Extracting cube roots to infinity,
An assignment for the boys
That will minimize noise   5
And produce a more peaceful vicinity.

25

Resistor, transistor, condensers in pairs,
Battery, platter, record me some airs;
Squeaker and squawker and woofer * times pi
And Baby shall have his own private Hi-Fi.

* *woofer:* The *Woofer*, as its name implies,
    Will sound the lows but not the highs.

21

JABBERWOCKY
Lewis Carroll

For our last bit of lyric laughter I offer the most famous nonsense poem in our language. And I've added the discussion of the poem as it occurs in *Through the Looking-Glass.*

'Twas brillig, and the slithy toves
   Did gyre and gimble in the wabe;
All mimsy were the borogoves,
   And the mome raths outgrabe.

"Beware the Jabberwock, my son!   5
   The jaws that bite, the claws that catch!
Beware the Jubjub bird, and shun
   The frumious Bandersnatch!"

He took his vorpal sword in hand:
   Long time the manxome foe he sought—   10
So rested he by the Tumtum tree,
   And stood awhile in thought.

And as in uffish thought he stood,
   The Jabberwock, with eyes of flame,
Came whiffling through the tulgey wood,   15
   And burbled as it came!

One, two! One, two! and through and through
   The vorpal blade went snicker-snack!
He left it dead, and with its head
   He went galumphing back.   20

"And hast thou slain the Jabberwock?
   Come to my arms, my beamish boy!
O frabjous day! Callooh! Callay!"
   He chortled in his joy.

22

'Twas brillig, and the slithy toves
   Did gyre and gimble in the wabe;
All mimsy were the borogoves,
   And the mome raths outgrabe.

"You seem very clever at explaining words, Sir," said Alice. "Would you kindly tell me the meaning of the poem called 'Jabberwocky'?"

"Let's hear it," said Humpty Dumpty. "I can explain all the poems that ever were invented—and a good many that haven't been invented just yet."

This sounded very hopeful, so Alice repeated the first verse:—

> " *'Twas brillig, and the slithy toves*
>   *Did gyre and gimble in the wabe:*
> *All mimsy were the borogoves,*
>   *And the mome raths outgrabe.*"

"That's enough to begin with," Humpty Dumpty interrupted: "there are plenty of hard words there. '*Brillig*' means four o'clock in the afternoon—the time when you begin *broiling* things for dinner."

"That'll do very well," said Alice: "and '*slithy*'?"

"Well, '*slithy*' means 'lithe and slimy.' 'Lithe' is the same as 'active.' You see it's like a portmanteau—there are two meanings packed up into one word."

"I see it now," Alice remarked thoughtfully: "and what are '*toves*'?"

"Well, '*toves*' are something like badgers—they're something like lizards—and they're something like corkscrews."

"They must be very curious-looking creatures."

"They are that," said Humpty Dumpty: "also they make their nests under sun-dials—also they live on cheese."

"And what's to '*gyre*' and to '*gimble*'?"

"To '*gyre*' is to go round and round like a gyroscope. To '*gimble*' is to make holes like a gimblet."

"And '*the wabe*' is the grass-plot round a sun-dial, I suppose?" said Alice, surprised at her own ingenuity.

"Of course it is. It's called 'wabe,' you know, because it goes a long way before it, and a long way behind it—"

"And a long way beyond it on each side," Alice added.

"Exactly so. Well then, 'mimsy' is 'flimsy and miserable' (there's another portmanteau for you). And a 'borogove' is a thin shabby-looking bird with its feathers sticking out all round —something like a live mop."

"And then 'mome raths'?" said Alice. "I'm afraid I'm giving you a great deal of trouble."

"Well, a 'rath' is a sort of green pig: but 'mome' I'm not certain about. I think it's short for 'from home'—meaning that they'd lost their way, you know."

"And what does 'outgrabe' mean?"

"Well, 'outgribing' is something between bellowing and whistling, with a kind of sneeze in the middle: however, you'll hear it done, maybe—down in the wood yonder—and, when you've once heard it, you'll be quite content. Who's been repeating all that hard stuff to you?"

"I read it in a book," said Alice.

Emotional Outlet and Growth

LYRIC VERSE can give you pleasure by providing an outlet for your emotions and a way of growing emotionally.

Emotions (anger, joy, love, hate, yearning, grief, and the like) are a vital part of our lives. They move within us and demand expression. If they are not given an outlet, various and sometimes serious difficulties, from temporary frustration to suicide, may result. So we find ways to express our emotions: blows with the fist, smiles, laughter, kisses, sobs. And *words:* from tender words of love to violent curses.

A distinguishing feature of most lyric verse is that it expresses emotions. It voices the author's personal feelings about something done, thought, seen, or heard. The poem becomes the poet's emotional release.

You, too, can find, and under emotional stress probably have found, release for your feelings in writing poetry. If, when you have sent flowers to a friend, you accompanied them with some bit of original verse, you were using poetry to help express your feelings. The flowers were not enough. You needed to get the emotion into words.

Since lyric poets, because of their keen sensitivities and their verbal skill, are more adept than you in expressing emotions, you may, rather than creating your own poems, sometimes turn to them for help in releasing your emotions. Upon reading some lyric poem, you may say, "Why, that's just the way I feel." That very declaration means that you have used the poet's words as an outlet for your emotion. And by storing up poems in your memory, you can richly equip yourself with a means of achieving emotional release in future "turns in your life." Moreover, the lyric poem has the power to recall a past emotional experience and to make you give that feeling a kind of second life. You cannot capture the intensity and immediateness of the first experience, but you take pleasure in reliving something of the same feeling and finally getting it expressed in words. Thus lyric poetry is able to serve your present, your future, and your past.

In addition to providing you with emotional release, lyric poetry can help you to grow emotionally. That is, it can increase your awareness of the range and intensity of emotions—from awe to jealousy to pity to remorse to love and hate. Probably no one individual ever experiences the whole gamut of emotions or all the degrees of intensity of any given emotion. By experiencing new and deeper emotions imaginatively through poetry, you can gain an understanding of the vital part emotions play in real life.

To summarize: emotions are an important part of your life, and they need release. One such means is the writing of poetry. If you cannot write it, you can become a reader of lyric verse and thereby find release for your emotions and a means of emotional growth.

A RED, RED ROSE
Robert Burns

Love between man and woman has moved many poets to write with warmth, sometimes with rapture, about the loved one. The following poem has long been a favorite of many readers.

> O my love is like a red, red rose,
>   That's newly sprung in June;
> O my love is like the melodie
>   That's sweetly played in tune.
>
> As fair art thou, my bonnie lass,   5
>   So deep in love am I;
> And I will love thee still, my dear,
>   Till a' the seas gang dry,

Till a' the seas gang dry, my dear,
And the rocks melt wi' the sun;   10
And I will love thee still, my dear,
While the sands o' life shall run.

And fare thee weel, my only love,
And fare thee weel awhile!
And I will come again, my love,   15
Though it were ten thousand mile!

Did this poem recall for you a pleasant memory of a former love?
Or did it put into words for you an emotion in your heart at the present
time? If it expresses an emotion you have not felt before, how did the
vicarious emotional experience you had in reading the poem make you
understand better what it means to be in love?

If the poem seems extravagantly exaggerated, what does this reaction
tell about your own experience with love?

Under what circumstances can you imagine yourself quoting this
poem to another? Why would you quote this instead of writing your
own poem? What other lyric, perhaps some popular song, might you
prefer to this poem as an expression of love?

HOW DO I LOVE THEE?

Elizabeth Barrett Browning

Among the love poems in the English language none is more
famous than the sonnets Elizabeth Barrett Browning wrote to express
her love for her husband, Robert Browning—also an important English
poet.

How do I love thee? Let me count the ways.
I love thee to the depth and breadth and height
My soul can reach, when feeling out of sight
For the ends of Being and ideal Grace.
I love thee to the level of everyday's   5
Most quiet need, by sun and candle-light.
I love thee freely, as men strive for Right;
I love thee purely, as they turn from Praise.
I love thee with the passion put to use
In my old griefs, and with my childhood's faith.   10

27

I love thee with a love I seemed to lose
With my lost saints,—I love thee with the breath,
Smiles, tears, of all my life!—and, if God choose
I shall but love thee better after death.

Which poem, Burns's or Mrs. Browning's, better expresses your own feelings (past or present)? Which poem would you prefer to have been written to you? What explanation can you give for this preference on your part? (Don't be too quick to distinguish between the poems because of the sex of the two poets.)

From which poem did you learn more of what it means to be in love? From your reading of each poem, what specific characteristics of love have you added to your knowledge of this emotion?

SEA LOVE

Charlotte Mew

The woman in this poem had an experience with love quite different from the one Mrs. Browning had. Even though these lovers once thought that their feelings were as enduring as the sea, their "love" turned out to be merely an infatuation. As you read this poem, be thinking what name you would give the feeling that comes through to you.

Tide be runnin' the great world over:
'Twas only last June month I mind that we
Was thinkin' the toss and the call in the breast of the lover
So everlastin' as the sea.

Heer's the same little fishes that sputter and swim,   5
Wi' the moon's old glim on the grey, wet sand;
An' him no more to me nor me to him
Than the wind goin' over my hand.

What feeling (one of sadness, or of regret, or of emptiness, or of bewilderment, or a combination of these or of others) do you think the poet is trying to express? How does the contrast between permanence and change help to express this feeling? What effect does the use of dialect have upon the expression of this feeling? In line 3, how do the words *toss* and *call* help to describe the vanished emotion?

If in your life you have had a similar emotional experience, try to describe poetically the feelings that such an event gave you.

28

MEXICAN SERENADE

Arthur Guiterman

In this poem the young señor exhibits a simple kind of joy in playing at the game of love, with which he is more in love than with Señorita Maraquita. The reader enjoys watching the young man at his game; and because he is able to smile at himself, he wins a kind of mild, pleasant admiration. Here is love with a light touch to give you a moment's amusement.

When the little armadillo
With his head upon the pillow
   Sweetly rests,
And the parakeet and lindo
Flitting past my cabin window   5
   Seek their nests,—

When the mists of evening settle
Over Popocatepetl,
   Dropping dew,—
Like the condor, brooding yonder,   10
Still I ponder, ever fonder
   Dear, of you!

May no revolution shock you,
May the earthquake gently rock you
   To repose,   15
While the sentimental panthers
Sniff the pollen-laden anthers
   Of the rose.

While the pelican is pining,
While the moon is softly shining   20
   On the stream,
May the song that I am singing
Send a tender cadence ringing
   Through your dream.

I have just one wish to utter,   25
That you twinkle through your shutter
    Like a star,
While according to convention,
I melodiously mention
    My guitar.   30

Señorita Maraquita,
Muy chiquita y bonita,
    Hear my lay!
But the dew is growing wetter
And perhaps you think I'd better   35
    Fade away.

1. *armadillo:* A burrowing, nocturnal animal having the body encased in
an armor of small bony plates.
4. *lindo:* Bright-colored South American tanager
8. *Popocatepetl:* Volcano, 30 miles west of Puebla, Mexico
17. *anthers:* The part of the stamen that contains the pollen
32. *Muy chiquita y bonita:* Very small and pretty (Spanish)
33. *lay:* song

For the ambitious student: Obtain in your school library information
about the courting customs in Mexico. Report to class. Which of these
conventions are included in this poem? What conventions in our society
play a part in the lives of young people courting one another?

NURSE

Frances Cornford

There are many kinds of love: the love when boy meets girl,
the love of our fellow man, the love of parents and children, the love
of country. This poem demonstrates a deep-felt affection for a child-
hood nurse, whose devotion to "her children," the poet believes, would
continue even after her death.

I cannot but believe, though you were dead,
Lying stone-still, and I came in, and said
(Having been out perhaps in storm and rain):—
"O dear, O look, I have torn my skirt again,"
That you would rise with the old simple ease,   5
And say, "Yes, child," and come to me.

And there
In your white crackling apron, on your knees,
With your quick hands, rough with the washing-up
Of every separate tended spoon and cup,
And with bent head, coiled with the happy hair   10
Your own child should have pulled for you (But no,
Your child who might have been, you did not bear,
Because the bottomless riches of your care
Were all for us) you would mend and heal my tear—
Mend, touch and heal; and stitching all the while,   15
Your cottons on your lap, look up and show
The sudden light perpetual of your smile—

And only then, you dear one, being dead
Go back and lie, like stone, upon your bed.

How would you name the emotion, or emotions, expressed in this
poem? For whom have you yourself ever felt similar emotions?

In whom have you ever seen traits so deeply embedded that you
could imagine them persisting after death? What was your emotional
attitude toward such characteristics? How has this poem changed your
attitude?

"BREATHES THERE THE MAN"
(from *Lay of the Last Minstrel*, Canto VI)
Walter Scott

In this poem Sir Walter Scott presents his emotional attitude
—a mixture of scorn and pity—toward a man who has no love for his
native country, whose heart remains indifferent to it upon returning
home after extensive foreign travel.

Breathes there the man, with soul so dead,
Who never to himself hath said,
This is my own, my native land!
Whose heart hath ne'er within him burned,
As home his footsteps he hath turned,   5
From wandering on a foreign strand!
If such there breathe, go, mark him well;

For him no Minstrel raptures swell;
High though his titles, proud his name,
Boundless his wealth as wish can claim,   10
Despite those titles, power, and pelf,
The wretch, concentered all in self,
Living, shall forfeit fair renown,
And, doubly dying, shall go down
To the vile dust, from whence he sprung,   15
Unwept, unhonored, and unsung.

The first six lines have become famous as an expression of love of
country. How did you react to them? Imagine yourself returning from
Europe. What would prompt you to recite these lines to yourself as you
glimpse the Statue of Liberty?

What emotion is expressed in lines 7–16? How would you express
the emotion aroused in you by a person who had no love for his native
land?

The U.S.A.—how much do you really love it? Write, in prose or
verse, about that love.

HOME THOUGHTS FROM ABROAD
Robert Browning

While living abroad in Italy, Robert Browning longed for his
homeland and especially for the emotional experience he associated
with being in England in the spring. Circumstances prevented his
returning. The expression of his emotion in words allowed him to relive
this emotional experience. Reading his poem will help you to under-
stand better how memories of little things can create poignant home-
sickness.

Oh, to be in England
Now that April's there,
And whoever wakes in England
Sees, some morning, unaware,
That the lowest boughs and the brushwood sheaf   5
Round the elm-tree bole are in tiny leaf,
While the chaffinch sings on the orchard bough
In England—now!

And after April, when May follows,
And the whitethroat builds, and all the swallows!   10

Hark, where my blossomed pear-tree in the hedge
Leans to the field and scatters on the clover
Blossoms and dewdrops—at the bent spray's edge—
That's the wise thrush; he sings each song twice over,
Lest you should think he never could recapture   15
The first fine careless rapture!
And though the fields look rough with hoary dew,
All will be gay when noontide wakes anew
The buttercups, the little children's dower
—Far brighter than this gaudy melon-flower!   20

6. *bole:* trunk
10. *whitethroat:* European warbler

What is the meaning of the last line? How does it add to the emotional effect of the poem?

What observations, if any, in Browning's poem have been experienced by you?

If you have ever been homesick, what or whom were you homesick to be with? What specific sense experiences (sight, smell, sound, taste, touch) do you ever long, with intensity of emotion, to repeat?

MY HEART LEAPS UP

William Wordsworth

Millions of human beings, from the inarticulate child to the wise elderly man, have been moved inwardly and outwardly when they have seen a rainbow. Wordsworth says that he is ready to die if the day should ever come when his heart will not respond to such a glorious sight. This event evokes in him not only a sensuous delight but also a reverence for a divine spirit pervading all nature.

My heart leaps up when I behold
    A rainbow in the sky:
So was it when my life began;
So is it now I am a man;
So be it when I shall grow old,   5
    Or let me die!
The Child is father of the Man;
And I could wish my days to be
Bound each to each by natural piety.

Once from a steamship in the Atlantic I saw a beautiful, complete double rainbow over the ocean. The grandeur of this phenomenon was almost unbearable. Involuntarily Wordsworth's little poem burst from my lips and brought me relief. Why don't you commit this little poem to memory and have it available if you should ever need it in the future?

FOUR LITTLE FOXES

Lew Sarett

In this poem the author realizes a certain helplessness on the part of man in solving the conflict between the forces of nature and animal life, and his pity and tenderness are aroused. But the weather to which the baby foxes are exposed can be harsh and cruel. The poet can only wish for nature to be tender, as he is.

Speak gently, Spring, and make no sudden sound;
For in my windy valley, yesterday I found
New-born foxes squirming on the ground—
   Speak gently.

Walk softly, March, forbear the bitter blow;   5
Her feet within a trap, her blood upon the snow,
The four little foxes saw their mother go—
   Walk softly.

Go lightly, Spring, oh, give them no alarm;
When I covered them with boughs to shelter them from harm, 10
The thin blue foxes suckled at my arm—
   Go lightly.

Step softly, March, with your rampant hurricane;
Nuzzling one another, and whimpering with pain,
The new little foxes are shivering in the rain—   15
   Step softly.

What would you have done if confronted by a similar situation? If in the future you are confronted with a situation of this kind, how different will be your emotions and actions because you have read this poem?

If your pity and tenderness toward animal life have been aroused some time during your life, write about that experience. Instill in the reader the emotions you had.

OLD IRONSIDES
Oliver Wendell Holmes

Oliver Wendell Holmes, a young man of twenty-one, became so aroused when he heard that the warship *Constitution* (War of 1812) was to be destroyed that he wrote the following poem. He sent it to the Boston *Advertiser,* where it was printed. The bitter, satirical tone in which the poem is presented is in direct opposition to the author's real affection for the ship. His method succeeded; readers of the poem were aroused; the ship was saved.

Ay, tear her tattered ensign down!
Long has it waved on high,
And many an eye has danced to see
That banner in the sky;
Beneath it rung the battle shout,   5
And burst the cannon's roar;—
The meteor of the ocean air
Shall sweep the clouds no more!

Her deck, once red with heroes' blood,
Where knelt the vanquished foe,   10
When winds were hurrying o'er the flood,
And waves were white below,
No more shall feel the victor's tread,
Or know the conquered knee;—
The harpies of the shore shall pluck   15
The eagle of the sea!

Oh, better that her shattered hulk
Should sink beneath the wave;
Her thunders shook the mighty deep,
And there should be her grave;   20

Nail to the mast her holy flag,
Set every threadbare sail,
And give her to the god of storms,
The lightning and the gale!

"Old Ironsides" has become a patriotic shrine located in Boston harbor and visited by thousands of tourists each year. Why, or why not, would you care to visit it? What other American shrine would you like to visit because you have read a lyric poem about it?

Practice reading the poem aloud to get across to the listener the full emotional impact. Do not overdramatize.

PIPPA'S SONG

(the heroine's song in *Pippa Passes*)

Robert Browning

Some poems represent emotional attitudes which poets take toward life as a whole. The next two poems present two such attitudes in sharp contrast.

The year's at the spring
And day's at the morn;
Morning's at seven;
The hillside's dew-pearled;
The lark's on the wing;   5
The snail's on the thorn:
God's in his heaven—
All's right with the world!

Why is it questionable interpretation to say of the last two lines, lifted from context, that they sum up the author's outlook on life?

A DIRGE *

Percy Bysshe Shelley

Rough wind, that moanest loud
Grief too sad for song;
Wild wind, when sullen cloud
Knells all the night long;

* A *dirge* is a kind of funeral song.

Sad storm, whose tears are vain, 5
Bare woods, whose branches strain,
Deep caves and dreary main,—
Wail, for the world's wrong!

What emotional effect is gained by using a number of nouns in direct address? In the last line do you think *world's* is a contraction or a possessive?

Explain under what circumstances you have felt the emotion expressed in either of these two poems. Show how each of these emotions can work constructively in your life.

LAMENT OF A MAN FOR HIS SON
(an adaptation of an American Indian lyric)
Mary Austin

The emotional responses to death vary considerably from person to person in attitude toward death itself, toward the person who has died, and toward the mourner's own self. Grief is frequently coupled with other emotions, for example self-pity. In this poem an American Indian father laments the loss of his son. Such a poem is called an *elegy*.*

Son, my son!

I will go up to the mountain
And there I will light a fire
To the feet of my son's spirit,
And there will I lament him; 5
Saying,
"O my son,
What is my life to me, now that you are departed!"

Son, my son,
In the deep earth 10
We softly laid thee in a chief's robe,
In a warrior's gear.
Surely there,
In the spirit land

* An *elegy* is a lyric poem setting forth the poet's meditation upon some solemn subject, usually death.

37

Thy deeds attend thee!   15
Surely,
The corn comes to ear again!

But I, here,
I am the stalk that the seed-gatherers
Descrying empty, afar, left standing.   20
Son, my son!
What is my life to me, now you are departed?

Whom does the father feel sorrier for, his son or himself? What
have you learned about grief from reading this poem?

DIRGE WITHOUT MUSIC

Edna St. Vincent Millay

Edna St. Vincent Millay reacts with unhappy resentment
against the very fact of death and how it robs her world of tender,
kind, beautiful living persons. She faces the fact of death boldly but
also rebels. You will find this feeling in strong contrast with that shown
in the Whitman poem which follows this one.

I am not resigned to the shutting away of loving hearts in the
        hard ground.
So it is, and so it will be, for so it has been, time out of mind:
Into the darkness they go, the wise and the lovely. Crowned
With lilies and with laurel they go; but I am not resigned.

Lovers and thinkers, into the earth with you.   5
Be one with the dull, the indiscriminate dust.
A fragment of what you felt, of what you knew,
A formula, a phrase remains,—but the best is lost.

The answers quick and keen, the honest look, the laughter, the
        love,—
They are gone. They have gone to feed the roses. Elegant and
        curled   10
Is the blossom. Fragrant is the blossom. I know. But I do not
        approve.

More precious was the light in your eyes than all the roses in the
world.

Down, down, down into the darkness of the grave
Gently they go, the beautiful, the tender, the kind;
Quietly they go, the intelligent, the witty, the brave.   15
I know. But I do not approve. And I am not resigned.

In your opinion what is the value of expressing the feeling of protest
against death? What does the phrase "without music" add to the title?

THE CAROL OF THE BIRD
(from *When Lilacs Last in the Dooryard Bloom'd*)
Walt Whitman

Like Miss Millay, Whitman faces up to the fact of death, but
his emotional attitude is quite opposite to hers. He accepts death, even
welcomes it. And death is pictured as a huge mother-image embracing
the dead one in comforting, solacing arms.

Come lovely and soothing death,
Undulate round the world, serenely arriving, arriving,
In the day, in the night, to all, to each,
Sooner or later delicate death.

Prais'd be the fathomless universe,   5
For life and joy, and for objects and knowledge curious,
And for love, sweet love—but praise! praise! praise!
For the sure-enwinding arms of cool-enfolding death.

Dark mother always gliding near with soft feet,
Have none chanted for thee a chant of fullest welcome?   10
Then I chant it for thee, I glorify thee above all,
I bring thee a song that when thou must indeed come, come un-
    falteringly.

Approach strong deliveress,
When it is so, when thou hast taken them I joyously sing the dead,

Lost in the loving floating ocean of thee,   15
Laved in the flood of thy bliss O death.

From me to thee glad serenades,
Dances for thee I propose saluting thee, adornments and feast-
    ings for thee,
And the sights of the open landscape and the high-spread sky are
    fitting,
And life and the fields, and the huge and thoughtful night.   20

The night in silence under many a star,
The ocean shore and the husky whispering wave whose voice I
    know,
And the soul turning to thee O vast and well-veil'd death,
And the body gratefully nestling close to thee.

Over the treetops I float thee a song,   25
Over the rising and sinking waves, over the myriad fields and the
    prairies wide,
Over the dense-pack'd cities all and the teeming wharves and
    ways,
I float this carol with joy, with joy to thee O death.

Explain why one of these two poems was the more comforting to
you than the other.

CROSSING THE BAR

Alfred Tennyson

Many poems express the poet's belief in a future life and the
comfort such a belief gives him in facing death. Of these none is more
famous than Tennyson's "Crossing the Bar." The poet asked that this
poem always conclude any selection of his poems, wherever published.

Sunset and evening star,
    And one clear call for me,
And may there be no moaning of the bar,
    When I put out to sea.

40

But such a tide as moving seems asleep,   5
   Too full for sound and foam,
When that which drew from out the boundless deep
   Turns again home.

Twilight and evening bell,
   And after that the dark!   10
And may there be no sadness of farewell,
   When I embark;

For tho' from out our bourne of time and place
   The flood may bear me far,
I hope to see my Pilot face to face   15
   When I have crossed the bar.

What is meant by "that which drew from out the boundless deep"?
Why is there sadness connected with death even among believers in
a future life?
What other poems about death do you know?

HIGH FLIGHT
John Gillespie Magee, Jr.

   Before the nineteen-year-old author of this poem was killed
in action in December of 1941, he had somehow found the time to
get into words his joy of conquering the air and manipulating a plane.
You will enjoy his boyish delight in his mastery and get a spiritual
lift from his wonder about man's accomplishment.

Oh, I have slipped the surly bonds of earth
And danced the skies on laughter-silvered wings;
Sunward I've climbed and joined the tumbling mirth
Of sun-split clouds—and done a hundred things
You have not dreamed of—wheeled and soared and swung   5
High in the sunlit silence. Hov'ring there,
I've chased the shouting wind along and flung
My eager craft through footless halls of air.
Up, up the long, delirious, burning blue
I've topped the wind-swept heights with easy grace,   10

41

Where never lark, or even eagle, flew;
And, while with silent, lifting mind I've trod
The high untrespassed sanctity of space,
Put out my hand, and touched the Face of God.

Explain whether or not you feel the author tempers his self-satisfaction with modesty.

Why do you think that a reader who has been up in the air might enjoy this poem more than the reader who has not had that experience?

UNTITLED

(from *Izaak Walton's Life of George Herbert*)

George Herbert

A young first-year student at Cambridge felt that if a poem could be the messenger of man's love for woman, even much more so could it serve as an expression of man's love for God. Earthly love must die; heavenly love endures.

My God, where is that ancient heat towards Thee
    Wherewith whole shoals of martyrs once did burn,
    Besides their other flames? Doth poetry
Wear Venus' livery, only to serve her turn?
Why are not sonnets made of Thee, and lays   5
    Upon Thine altar burnt? Cannot Thy love
    Heighten a spirit to sound out Thy praise
As well as any she? Cannot Thy Dove
Outstrip their Cupid easily in flight?
    Or since Thy ways are deep and still the same,   10
    Will not a verse run smooth that bears Thy name?
Why doth that fire, which by Thy power and might
    Each breast does feel, no braver fuel choose
    Than that which one day worms may chance refuse?

2. *shoals:* throngs
4. *Venus:* goddess of love and beauty
5. *lays:* songs

To what extent was this poem an outlet for your own emotion? To what extent did it provide you with a vicarious emotional experience which increased your knowledge of emotions?

Music in Words

LYRIC VERSE can give you pleasure through its music —the music of sound-patterns in words.

It is true that a number of poems have been set to music or have been given musical settings. But that music is something in addition to the music of carefully chosen words arranged in certain patterns of rhythm and other sound effects.

Rhythm

An essential of all poetry is *rhythm*. Inherently pleasurable to man as rhythm is, it is not easy to define. You and I sense it in the world about us: in the tides of the ocean, in the movement of the stars, in the change from night to day, in the rotation of the seasons, in breathing, even in the ordering of the lengths of the thumb and fingers on the hand. We notice it, too, in speech, in the phonetic movement of words with their accented and unaccented syllables. And in reading poetry (which, as you know, must be read aloud), you learn to catch the rhythm of a particular poem, from the rough-shod beat of an ancient and primitive chant to the tuxedoed accents of a sophisticated modern song. Whether it is an easy lilt or a brittle zip or a stately step, you come to sense the pulse and beat, the sweep of phrase, the overall rise and fall that the poet has created for your pleasure by his organization of sound-patterns in words.

The formal organization of accented and unaccented syllables into definite, regular patterns is called *meter*. The unit of meter is the *metrical foot*.

Here are five words divided into syllables.

above —a bove′
dinner —din′ ner
introduce—in tro duce′
merrily —mer′ ri ly
bowwow —bow′ wow′

Each word consists of two or more syllables, with certain syllables accented, or stressed. By making a ′ sign above the stressed syllables and a ∪ sign above the unstressed syllables, these five words can represent the basic metrical feet.

WORD	NAME OF METER	NAME OF FOOT	DIAGRAM
above	iambic	iamb	∪ ′
dinner	trochaic	trochee	′ ∪
introduce	anapestic	anapest	∪ ∪ ′
merrily	dactylic	dactyl	′ ∪ ∪
bowwow	spondaic	spondee	′ ′

A line of poetry consists of a number of metrical feet. If the basic pattern is iambic (∪ ′) and there is only one such foot in a line, the line is called iambic *monometer*.

1
Ĭf Í |
1
Coŭld flý.| . .

Whatever the major meter (iambic, trochaic, etc.) may be, a line made up of two metrical feet is known as *dimeter*; of three, *trimeter;* of four, *tetrameter;* of five, *pentameter;* of six, *hexameter;* of seven, *heptameter*. Some examples are:

spondaic monometer

1
Drínk — Brínk — |
1
Foúnd Drowńed. |
—*G. W. Brodribb*

iambic dimeter

1 2
Thĕ Dél|ŭge drówn'd
1 2
Thĕ Eárth | ărоúnd.
—*New England Primer*

<table>
<tr><td>trochaic
trimeter</td><td>

1   2   3

Mórtal | mán and | wóman, |

1   2   3

Go úp|on your | trável! |

—*E. B. Browning*
</td></tr>
</table>

<table>
<tr><td>anapestic
tetrameter</td><td>

1   2   3   4

They're not é|pics, but thát | dóesn't mát|ter a pín, |

1   2   3   4

In créa|ting, the ón|ly hárd thing's | to begín. |

—*J. R. Lowell*
</td></tr>
</table>

<table>
<tr><td>iambic
pentameter</td><td>

1   2   3   4   5

Avénge, | O Lórd, | thy sláugh|tered sáints, | whose
bónes |

1   2   3   4   5

Lie scát|tered ón | the Ál|pine moun|tains cóld |. . .

—*John Milton*
</td></tr>
</table>

<table>
<tr><td>dactylic
hexameter</td><td>

1   2   3   4

Thís is the | fórest prim|éval; but | whére are the |

5   6

héarts that be|néath it |

1   2   3

Léaped like the | róe, when he | héars in the | wóod-

4   5   6

land the | vóice of the | húntsman. . .

—*H. W. Longfellow*
</td></tr>
</table>

In poems variations of these formal metrical rhythms are not only possible but highly desirable, because variations prevent the mechanical effect and monotony of a too-regular beat. The poet must not become a slave to meter.

Variations can be gained by substituting one metrical foot for another. For example, if the prevailing meter is iambic ($\smallsmile$ ′), an anapest ($\smallsmile$ $\smallsmile$ ′), a spondee (′ ′), or even a trochee (′ $\smallsmile$) may be substituted. (In the foregoing example of dactylic hexameter, you will have noticed the substitution in the sixth foot.) Another

45

way to prevent monotony is to make a pause in the thought at some place other than at the end of the line. Lines in which the thought continues into the next line are referred to as *run-on lines.*

Let us read some poems that are strongly metrical. First, read the selections through to get the main thought, mood, and feeling. Then read the selection aloud. Be conscious of the rhythm. But watch, especially when the meter is very pronounced, that you do not destroy the meaning by giving undue emphasis to the accented and unaccented syllables. Meter is but the bones of poetry; rhythm and emotion and thought are the flesh and blood. At no time must the bones push through the flesh in the oral rendition. You want to enjoy the music and its emotional effect without missing what the poet has to say.

YOUNG AND OLD
Charles Kingsley

The meter in this poem is regular with the exception of a pause substituted for the unaccented syllable in the iamb containing *lad,* a noun in direct address. (Note the contrast in ideas between the two parts of the poem.)

<pre>
       1   2   3   4
When all | the world | is young, | lad, | 4
     1   2   3
And all | the trees | are green; | 3
And ev|'ry goose | a swan, | lad, | 4
  And ev|'ry lass | a queen; | 3
Then hey | for boot | and horse, | lad, | 4   5
  And round | the world | away; | 3
Young blood | must have | its course, | lad | 4
  And ev|'ry dog | his day. | 3
</pre>

When all the world is old, lad,
  And all the trees are brown;   10

46

And all the sport is stale, lad,
And all the wheels run down;
Creep home, and take your place there,
The spent and maimed among:
God grant you find one face there,   15
You loved when all was young.

Note that though the mood changes in the second part, the meter does not. How would you indicate orally this contrast in ideas and moods? What would your reaction be to a very slow oral reading of the second stanza?

A VAGABOND SONG

Bliss Carman

This poem has a haunting and infectious rhythm—one that gets into the bloodstream. You naturally want to say the poem aloud so that you can enjoy the music in the words.

      1   2   3   4   5   6

There is some|thing in | the au|tumn that | is na|tive to | my

    7

blood— |

    1   2   3

Touch of man|ner, hint | of mood; |

    1   2   3

And my heart | is like | a rhyme, |

    1   2   3   4   5   6

With the yel|low and | the pur|ple and | the crim|son keep|ing

    7

time. |

The scarlet of the maples can shake me like a cry   5
Of bugles going by.
And my lonely spirit thrills
To see the frosty asters like a smoke upon the hills.

47

There is something in October sets the gypsy blood astir;
We must rise and follow her,   10
When from every hill of flame
She calls and calls each vagabond by name.

What kind of music does the rhythm recall? Along with the pictures
presented, what emotion did the rhythm arouse in you? I suggest
that you memorize this poem. Under what circumstances would it be
pleasurable to recall it, even to recite it from memory?

SONG FOR A FIFTH CHILD

Ruth H. Hamilton

There is in this poem a rhythmical playfulness wholly in
keeping with the content. A mother of five has much cleaning and
feeding and washing to do, but she does not allow these small cares
to interfere with her "blissfully rocking" the fifth child to sleep. The
playfulness suggests that the meter will have considerable variety,
more so than the two preceding poems have.

Mother, oh mother, come shake out your cloth!
Empty the dustpan, poison the moth,
Hang out the washing and butter the bread,
Sew on a button and make up a bed.
Where is the mother whose house is so shocking?   5
She's up in the nursery, blissfully rocking!

Oh, I've grown as shiftless as Little Boy Blue
  (Lullaby, rockaby, lullaby loo).
Dishes are waiting and bills are past due
  (Pat-a-cake, darling, and peek, peekaboo).   10
The shopping's not done and there's nothing for stew
And out in the yard there's a hullabaloo
But I'm playing Kanga and this is my Roo.   [Remember *Winnie*
Look! Aren't her eyes the most wonderful hue?   *the Pooh?*]
  (Lullaby, rockaby, lullaby loo.)   15

Oh, cleaning and scrubbing will wait till tomorrow,
But children grow up, as I've learned to my sorrow.
So quiet down, cobwebs. Dust, go to sleep.
I'm rocking my baby. Babies don't keep.

48

If you did not feel the rocker rocking, you should read the poem again.

What kind of a person do you think the mother is?

A note from the author states that "out of a total of nineteen lines, ten are clearly dactylic." Do you agree? What meters are used in the other ten lines?

Rime and Alliteration

A poet often adds to the music of a poem by using two well-known devices: rime and alliteration.

Rime

Rime is the repetition of the same vowel and consonant sounds in different arrangements. It usually occurs at the ends of lines of poetry, but there is also internal rime, which comes within the line. Here are four of the methods of riming.

NAME	EXPLANATION	EXAMPLE
masculine rime	The initial consonants of final stressed syllables vary.	night fight
		deranged changed
feminine rime	The initial consonants of stressed syllables vary, with the stressed syllables followed by one or two identical unaccented syllables.	swinging ringing
		tenderly slenderly
assonance (near rime)	The vowel sounds are the same; the initial consonants may vary; the end consonants vary.	cold boat
		neck net
consonance (near rime)	The end consonants are the same; the vowel sounds vary.	bite boot
		hazed dozed

Alliteration

Alliteration, really a variation of rime, is the repetition of the same sound (usually a consonant) that begins stressed syllables within a line of poetry. Note the following four examples.

1. *P*ale, beyond *p*orch and *p*ortal . . .
2. *W*an *w*aves and *w*et *w*inds labor . . .
3. And *d*evils to a*d*ore for *d*eities . . .
4. An Austrian *a*rmy, *a*wfully *a*rrayed . . .

MONEY

Richard Armour

This popular poem, in trochaic (′ ◡) dimeter, makes clever use of a kind of feminine rime, as if the unaccented *it* and the preceding stressed syllable were parts of the same word. I am sure you will agree with the statement in the last line.

Wórkers | eárn ĭt, |	a
Spéndthrifts | búrn ĭt, |	a
Bankers lend it,	b
Women spend it,	b
Forgers fake it,	c 5
Taxes take it,	c
Dying leave it,	d
Heirs receive it,	d
Thrifty save it,	e
Misers crave it,	e 10
Robbers seize it,	f
Rich increase it,	f (assonance)
Gamblers lose it . . .	g
I could use it.	g

11-12. Or does the author want to give a light touch to the poem by having the *s* in *increase* pronounced like a *z*?

LONE DOG

Irene Rutherford McLeod

This poem, which has an insistent rhythm that seems to be a very part of the character of the dog portrayed, contains both end and internal rime. The meter is prevailingly iambic, salted with a number of anapests.

I'm a lean | dog, a keen | dog, a wild | dog, and lone; | x x   a
I'm a rough | dog, a tough | dog, hunt|ing on | my own; | y y   a
I'm a bad | dog, a mad | dog, teas|ing sil|ly sheep; | z z   b
I love | to sit | and bay | the moon, | to keep | fat souls |
    from sleep. | b

I'll never be a lap dog, licking dirty feet,   5
A sleek dog, a meek dog, cringing for my meat,
Not for me the fireside, the well-filled plate,
But shut door, and sharp stone, and cuff and kick and hate.

Not for me the other dogs, running by my side,
Some have run a short while, but none of them would bide.   10
O mine is still the lone trail, the hard trail, the best,
Wide wind, and wild stars, and hunger of the quest!

Why do you feel the poem would be more, or less, effective by the omission of the internal rimes? Find examples of alliteration in this poem.

What emotion, if any, did the poem arouse in you? Understanding the character of the dog, do you feel it would ever become somebody's pet? Even though this poem is about an animal, what relation do you see to human beings?

LIKE RAIN IT SOUNDED TILL IT CURVED

Emily Dickinson

In this poem excellent use is made of consonance (see lines 2 and 4, 9 and 11, 10 and 12, 14 and 16). Your own experience with storms sets the stage for your enjoyment of this poem. Note the progression of the storm. The formal meter and the carefully chosen words enhance the description as if in direct contrast to the erratic rhythm and the coarse vocabulary of a storm.

> Like rain it sounded till it curved,
> And then I knew 'twas wind;
> It walked as wet as any wave
> But swept as dry as sand.
> When it had pushed itself away   5
> To some remotest plain,
> A coming as of hosts was heard—
> That was indeed the rain!
> It filled the wells, it pleased the pools,
> It warbled in the road,   10
> It pulled the spigot from the hills
> And let the floods abroad;
> It loosened acres, lifted seas,
> The sites of centers stirred,
> Then like Elijah rode away   [See II Kings 2:9–12] 15
> Upon a wheel of cloud.

Find examples of alliteration. Which of these did you especially enjoy?

What kind of pacing does a good oral reading of this poem demand?

Try your poetical hand in describing a storm, one from your own experience. I hope that some of the simple directness and careful diction demonstrated in this poem rub off into your own writing.

Music without Meter and Rime

Free Verse

There are ways other than meter and rime by which the poet may musically integrate his thought and feeling. One of these is *free verse,* or *vers libre,* a pattern not easy to define and difficult to write well. Good free verse is not merely prose broken up into lines of unequal length. Although the syllables of the words are not organized into a formal meter of repeated stresses at regular intervals, the wording is most carefully selected. The lines build up an uneven but rhythmic flow called *cadence.* Read the following example.

BY THE BIVOUAC'S FITFUL FLAME
Walt Whitman

The rather slow measured rhythm is appropriate to the solemn, brooding mood of this poem. It is concerned with the poet's own experience during the Civil War.

By the bivouac's fitful flame,
A procession winding around me, solemn and sweet and slow—
    but first I note,
The tents of the sleeping army, the fields' and woods' dim outline,
The darkness lit by spots of kindled fire, the silence,
Like a phantom far or near an occasional figure moving,   5
The shrubs and trees, (as I lift my eyes they seem to be stealthily
    watching me,)
While wind in procession thoughts, O tender and wondrous
    thoughts,
Of life and death, of home and the past and loved, and of those
    that are far away;
A solemn and slow procession there as I sit on the ground,
By the bivouac's fitful flame.   10

In this poem what kinds of repetition help to create music in words?

THE BEAT CHILD
Chuck Stoddard

This is a bit of free verse written by a high-school boy. His teacher says, " 'The Beat Child' was written by a boy who arrived in my class by the circuitous route of several other English classes, where, each time, his tenure was brief and his retirement a relief. Is this poetry? Maybe not, but I rather think so."

Who are you, oh misled child
That searches for nothing?
You look by day,
And spend your nights thinking,
But still searching for nothing.
Most people would call you beat,

53

Others a juvenile delinquent.
I'd say you were lost,
But you'd say you're found.
Found in a life of mystery,
Lost in finding an answer.
Your life is spent in a gas house
With others who are searching,
Searching for the purpose;
The purpose of living
Our ungodly life.

What is your opinion? "Is this poetry?"

Anglo-Saxon Verse Form

Another substitute for formal meter and rime is that form used centuries ago by the Anglo-Saxons. The line of poetry is divided into halves by a pause,* each half containing two stresses. In other words, the line contains four accented syllables and an indefinite number of unaccented ones. Alliteration accompanies this rhythm. The following example shows how a contemporary poet employs this form.

LONDON TRAIN

Paul Dehn

Snoring in a Smoker, || soot-cratered from Stockport,
I awoke to find Warwickshire || under a wintry sky
Leaden to my left || in the late afternoon
But, on my right, embered in the early evening;
Mounting among whose mists at the milk-white hour   5
Stood trees trim as spires and a spire tree-tall,
Whose tops skimmed the skyline like a school of fishes
Or ducked into darkness under a down's wave.
And all swam so sweetly to the train's swaying,
To the deep drone and the din of the wheels   10

* The technical name for such a pause (and other similar pauses) is caesura.

That I fell to drowsing, and woke adrift
In a mean city of Man's making
Sootier than Stockport, under no stars.

(For other examples of Anglo-Saxon verse form see pp. 187 and 222.)

Syllabic Verse

A third way, one not commonly used, to achieve music without formal metrical stress and with or without rime is to establish forms by syllables alone. The poetic line is determined by the number of syllables—not by the number of words or by metrical feet. The little pattern that follows, called a *cinquain* (pronounced *sing-káne*), was created by the author herself.

TRIAD
Adelaide Crapsey

	SYLLABLES
These be	2
Three silent things:	4
The falling snow . . . the hour	6
Before the dawn . . . the mouth of one	8
Just dead.	2

The cinquain reminds one of a form that has been recently revived and that comes to us from Japanese poetry. A *hokku* is a little poem made up of seventeen syllables so portioned that the first line contains five syllables; the second, seven; and the third, five. The following hokku about marriage is by Chiyo (translated by Curtis Hidden Page).

The persimmon, lo!	5
None can tell till he tastes it!	7
Even so, marriage.	5

Why not try to write your own cinquain or hokku? (Be sure that you have something to say.)

Stanza Forms

The lines of many poems are arranged into regular units with a space separating the units. For example, one poem that consists of twelve lines is divided into six sets of two lines; another, into four sets of three lines; another into three sets of four lines; still another, into two sets of six lines. Each of these sets constitutes a *stanza*,* with the metrical pattern that has been established in the first stanza repeated in the following stanzas. There may be a rime scheme. If so, it is also repeated. And, of course, what has been said about metrical variations, even in fairly rigid patterns, applies to stanzas, too.

There are a number of stanzaic patterns, and every poet is free to create new ones. One of the most frequently used is the *quatrain*, a stanza of four lines. Within this classification is the *common measure*, or hymnal stanza. It is like the old ballad (narrative poetry) stanza but strictly regular and iambic (˘ ′) in meter with the rime (represented by the letters) and the foot pattern (represented by the numbers) running a4 b3 c4 b3 or a4 b3 a4 b3. Note the example.

<pre>
   1   2   3   4
Ŏ Gód, | oŭr hélp | ĭn á|gĕs pást, | a4

   1   2   3
Oŭr hópe | fŏr yéars | tŏ cóme, | b3

   1   2   3   4
Oŭr shĕl|tĕr fróm | thĕ stór|mў blást, | a4

   1   2   3
Ănd óur | ĕtér|năl hóme: | b3
</pre>

Another popular form of the quatrain, sometimes referred to as the *heroic quatrain*, is a four-line stanza of iambic (˘ ′) pentameter riming a b a b. An example follows. It is the opening stanza of Thomas Gray's very famous and well-known poem, "Elegy Written in a Country Churchyard."

* When you mean *stanza*, say *stanza*. A *verse* is a single line of poetry. "The popular use of *verse* in the sense of *stanza* is contrary to the best usage," says Webster.

56

The cur|few tolls | the knell | of part|ing day, | a5
The lowing herd wind slowly o'er the lea,   b5
The plowman homeward plods his weary way   a5
And leaves the world to darkness and to me.   b5

For practical purposes, the shortest stanza is the two-liner, which is called a *couplet* when the lines rime. If the couplet consists of two lines of rimed iambic pentameter, it is called a *heroic couplet*. The following two examples are by Alexander Pope, a master of this pattern.

Fear not | the an|ger of | the wise | to raise; | a5
Those best | can bear | reproof, | who mer|it praise.| a5

Regard not then if wit be old or new,   a5
But blame the false, and value still the true.   a5

The couplet, of course, frequently joins other couplets to form a poem with no stanzaic divisions.

Let's read some complete poems that demonstrate certain stanzaic patterns.

GOLDEN BOUGH

Elinor Wylie

This poem illustrates the heroic quatrain. It describes the way a poet saw and felt a "golden" autumn, distinguished by the glorious color of the leaves.

These lovely groves of fountain-trees that shake
A burning spray against autumnal cool
Descend again in molten drops to make
The rutted path a river and a pool.

They rise in silence, fall in quietude,   5
Lie still as looking-glass to every sense
Save where their lion-color in the wood
Roars to miraculous heat and turbulence!

Review the definition of the heroic quatrain and show that this poem fulfills the requirements of the definition.

In what way did this poem make you see autumn anew? What emotion did the poem arouse in you?

What qualities does this poem have in common with Emily Dickinson's poem on page 51? Compare this poem about autumn with the one by Bliss Carman on page 47.

IN A GARDEN

(with the usual apologies)

Donald C. Babcock

This little poem is written in couplets. You will find in it not only rhythmical gracefulness but also keen observation plus some serious thinking about that observation.

> I think that I shall never make
> A poem sinuous as a snake:
>
> A snake that can us mammals mock
> Whenas he moves upon a rock;
>
> Whose muscular and graceful strength   5
> Dwells in the one dimension, length;
>
> Who has no radiating limb
> And yet on waves of land can swim;
>
> Who can from raspberry vines and air
> Devise himself a rocking-chair;   10
>
> Who worships silent in the sun;
> Who has no projects to be done;
>
> Who thinks no thought, who makes no sound,
> Preferring to remain profound;
>
> Who, though from dust he scarce can rise,   15
> Appropriates man's paradise.

I strive, like Adam, every spring,
To conjure that elusive thing,

An Eden, with my hoe and rake:
The Serpent only God could make.   20

Do you find the couplet pleasing to your ear? If you don't, what do
you think is the reason?

O GOD OUR HELP IN AGES PAST

Isaac Watts

You yourself have perhaps sung this famous hymn, written
in common measure. Now you have a chance to test the power of the
words themselves—without the musical accompaniment.

O God, our help in ages past,
Our hope for years to come,
Our shelter from the stormy blast,
And our eternal home:

Under the shadow of thy throne   5
Thy saints have dwelt secure;
Sufficient is thine arm alone,
And our defense is sure.

Before the hills in order stood,
Or earth received her frame,   10
From everlasting thou art God,
To endless years the same.

A thousand ages in thy sight
Are like an evening gone;
Short as the watch that ends the night   15
Before the rising sun.

Time, like an ever-rolling stream,
Bears all its sons away;

They fly, forgotten, as a dream
Dies at the opening day.   20

O God, our help in ages past,
Our hope for years to come,
Be thou our guide while life shall last,
And our eternal home.

What, if any, slight deviations from the common measure did you notice?
Find other examples of consonance like that in lines 2 and 4.
What is the portrait of God given in this hymn? Make a statement as to the meaning of the poem. What is the prevailing mood?
What other hymns do you especially enjoy? Tell why.

THREE WOULDS

Anonymous

To enjoy this clever little whimsey, you need to be familiar with the common measure. The fun comes in the last line of each stanza, a delightful variation on a much-used stanzaic pattern.

I would I were beneath a tree,
A-sleeping in the shade,
With all the bills I've got to pay
Paid!

I would I were beside the sea,   5
Or sailing in a boat,
With all the things I've got to write
Wrote!

I would I were on yonder hill,
A-basking in the sun   10
With all the things I've got to do
Done!

In the last line of the second stanza, the poet is being ungrammatical on purpose.* Why does this error succeed in this poem whereas it might be disastrous in other poems?

* Such deviations are called *poetic license.*

Blank Verse

You may recall, from your study of Shakespeare for example, that blank verse usually refers to poetry written in unrimed iambic pentameter. Being a very flexible form, it is used extensively in narrative and dramatic poetry. In lyric poetry blank verse is apt to be employed in a fairly lengthy descriptive or meditative poem.

THE SNOW-STORM
Ralph Waldo Emerson

Announced by all the trumpets of the sky,
Arrives the snow, and, driving o'er the fields,
Seems nowhere to alight: the whited air
Hides hills and woods, the river, and the heaven,
And veils the farm-house at the garden's end.   5
The sled and traveller stopped, the courier's feet
Delayed, all friends shut out, the housemates sit
Around the radiant fireplace, enclosed
In a tumultuous privacy of storm.

Come see the north wind's masonry.   10
Out of an unseen quarry evermore
Furnished with tile, the fierce artificer
Curves his white bastions with projected roof
Round every windward stake, or tree, or door.
Speeding, the myriad-handed, his wild work   15
So fanciful, so savage, nought cares he
For number or proportion. Mockingly,
On coop or kennel he hangs Parian wreaths;
A swan-like form invests the hidden thorn;
Fills up the farmer's lane from wall to wall,   20
Maugre the farmer's sighs; and at the gate
A tapering turret overtops the work.
And when his hours are numbered, and the world
Is all his own, retiring, as he were not,

Leaves, when the sun appears, astonished Art
To mimic in slow structures, stone by stone,
Built in an age, the mad wind's nightwork,
The frolic architecture of the snow.

18. *Parian:* Paros was noted for its beautiful marble.
21. *maugre:* in spite of

Practice reading this poem aloud. You must not read blank verse line by line. Grasp the flow of thought, which often continues into the next line. Blank verse very definitely has rhythm, but you must not make it sing-songish. Sense the metrical variety within the regularity.

The Sonnet

The sonnet is a complete poem of fourteen iambic pentameter lines, which are traditionally divided into the first eight (the octave) and into the last six (the sestet). Often when the sonnet appears on the printed page, it is divided into units. This practice gives the impression of stanzas although, strictly speaking, these divisions are not true stanzas. The rime schemes vary according to the traditional plan which the poet selects. The following chart is intended to serve as a convenient summary of and guide to these facts.

| | Two waves of thought | |
| | Main thought or rising emotion | Question, hope, yearning, resolved |
NAME	OCTAVE	SESTET
Italian or Petrarchan	a b b a a b b a	c d e c d e c d c d c d
Shakespearean	a b a b c d c d	e f e f g g
Spenserian	a b a b b c b c	c d c d e e
Miltonic	like the Italian but without the strict thought division	

The sonnet, in former times, was dedicated to the object of the poet's affection, but the range of subject matter in the sonnet today is almost unlimited. Poets, through use and experimentation, have kept the form alive and vigorous.

SONNET 29

William Shakespeare

It is good to discover that the persons whom you learn to accept as great have once been real people, with problems and shortcomings. Shakespeare knew what it was to be dispirited and downhearted, even envious of the green grass in the other person's yard. But love snapped him out of his black mood.

When, in disgrace with fortune and men's eyes,
I all alone beweep my outcast state,
And trouble deaf heaven with my bootless cries,
And look upon myself and curse my fate,
Wishing me like to one more rich in hope,   5
Featured like him, like him with friends possessed,
Desiring this man's art and that man's scope,
With what I most enjoy contented least;
Yet in these thoughts myself almost despising,
Haply I think on thee,—and then my state,   10
Like to the lark at break of day arising
From sullen earth, sings hymns at heaven's gate;
For thy sweet love remembered such wealth brings
That then I scorn to change my state with kings.

ALL THAT MATTERS

Edgar A. Guest

When I was a child, God was pictured to me as a great bookkeeper of thoughts and deeds. I even recall some old, crude but effective illustrations of a huge book open across an ancient man's knees; he had pen in hand and was about to write. This poem makes use of that notion and its relation to the fact of death—and life.

When all that matters shall be written down
And the long record of our years is told,
Where sham, like flesh, must perish and grow cold;
When the tomb closes on our fair renown

And priest and layman, sage and motleyed clown   5
Must quit the places which they dearly hold,
What to our credit shall we find enscrolled?
And what shall be the jewels of our crown?
I fancy we shall hear to our surprise
Some little deeds of kindness, long forgot,   10
Telling our glory, and the brave and wise
Deeds which we boasted often, mentioned not.
God gave us life not just to buy and sell,
And all that matters is to live it well.

TO A PHOTOGRAPHER
Berton Braley

Read this sonnet to see whether or not you have been the victim of the too-flattering photographer.

I have known love and hate and work and fight;
I have lived largely, I have dreamed and planned,
And Time, the Sculptor, with a master hand
Has graven on my face for all men's sight
Deep lines of joy and sorrow, growth and blight   5
Of labor and of service and command
—And now you show me this, this waxen, bland
And placid face, unlined, unwrinkled, white.

This is not I—this fatuous thing you show,
Retouched and smoothed and prettified to please,   10
Put back the wrinkles and the lines I know;
I have spent blood and tears achieving these,
Out of the pain, the struggle and the wrack
These are my scars of battle—put them back!

By which of these sonnets were you most aroused emotionally? Intellectually? Which of the sonnets comes closest to describing emotions and thoughts you have experienced? Under what conditions did you experience these?

To what extent does each of these sonnets conform to the explanation given about sonnets (subject matter, meter, rime, thought division, lyric quality)?

Memorize the one you like the best and come to class prepared to write it exactly right.

Sharpened Sense Antennae

LYRIC VERSE can give you pleasure by sharpening the antennae of your five senses: sight, sound, smell, taste, touch.

Sense Impressions in Words

Through the activities of the five senses, you have stored up in your mind what are called sense impressions. Perhaps you can recall the beautiful lone oak tree in the pasture (sight), the crunch * of dried leaves under your feet (sound), the aroma of popping corn (smell), the tang of cider (taste), and the first bee sting (touch). Such sense impressions are called *images*. We all collect and file in our minds, ready for reference, these images obtained through the five senses.

The poet—by talent, by experience, by reading, by trial-and-error—is particularly good at collecting images. His sensibilities are exceptionally alive, alert, tingling with the small excitements and stimulating thoughts round about him. He "looks at a tree until it appears to him as a tree appears to every one else, and then he looks at it till he sees what no man has seen before." And he wants to share that discovery with you and me, who, let us admit, have often rather lazily allowed our senses to go unsharpened.

The poet is also a shrewd manipulator of words, almost a magician. He has a special ability to put his sense impressions

* The use of a word the sound of which suggests its meaning is called *onomatopoeia;* e.g., *crunch, hiss, buzz, bowwow.*

(images) into words. These images-in-words we call *imagery*. Through imagery the poet transfers his sense impressions to the reader. By means of this communication through imagery, the poet can help you to become more keenly aware of the splendors about you.

IMAGE IN POET'S MIND

"The squirrel, with raised paws, and form erect"

IMAGE IN YOUR MIND

IMAGE-IN-WORDS
(IMAGERY)

To get what the poet has put into a poem, you must read alertly. True response to the imagery means that you actively recreate the images. If the poet wants you to smell the balsam of a Christmas tree, smell it. If the poet wants you to get the feel of a kitten's soft fur, feel it. If the poet wants you to see the colors of a stained-glass window, be sure that you see that image completely. Use your imagination. It will help you to transfer the images-in-words into vivid images in your own mind. Unless you do that, you are not reading alertly. And if, in the course of your reading, you recognize that some of the poet's images correspond to some in your storehouse of sense impressions, you will experience the pleasure of recognition and happy memory. You will also take delight in the imagery that is fresh and novel. But you must read with all the organ stops of your imagination open. Active and zealous practice will increase your ability to enjoy the richness that exists in the world of sense experience: sights, smells, feels, tastes, and sounds.

BARTER

Sara Teasdale

As you read this poem, relive the sensations. In your mind actually see, hear, smell, feel! Take delight in discovering which images of the "beautiful and splendid things" are to you pleasant memories and which are new experiences. (Before you start reading, you might ask yourself about the meaning of the word *barter* used as the title.)

Life has loveliness to sell,
All beautiful and splendid things,
Blue waves whitened on a cliff,　　　　　[Sight
Soaring fire that sways and sings,　　　　and
And children's faces looking up　　　　　Sound.]　5
Holding wonder like a cup.

Life has loveliness to sell,
Music like a curve of gold,　　　　　[Sound and sight.]
Scent of pine trees in the rain,　　　　[Smell.]
Eyes that love you, arms that hold,　　[Sight and touch.]　10
And for your spirit's still delight,
Holy thoughts that star the night.

Spend all you have for loveliness,
Buy it and never count the cost;
For one white singing hour of peace　　[Peace of mind.]　15
Count many a year of strife well lost,
And for a breath of ecstasy
Give all you have been, or could be.

To what extent did the poem convince you of life's loveliness? What is the poet indicating by the exaggerations, especially those in the last stanza?

Which image did you find the most novel? Which of the items of "loveliness" are not literal sense impressions?

What stanzaic pattern has the author used (number of lines, meter, and rime)?

LOVELIEST OF TREES

A. E. Housman

Take a second look at that cherry tree in your back yard.
Have you fully caught its beauty? You are not here on earth forever,
and to live means, in part, daily to enjoy the beauty in the world
around us. The poet admonishes you and me to make the most of such
opportunities.

Loveliest of trees, the cherry now
Is hung with bloom along the bough,
And stands about the woodland ride
Wearing white for Eastertide.

Now, of my threescore years and ten,   5
Twenty will not come again,
And take from seventy springs a score,
It only leaves me fifty more.

And since to look at things in bloom
Fifty springs are little room,   10
About the woodlands I will go
To see the cherry hung with snow.

SMELLS

Christopher Morley

The title is self-explanatory. Go right ahead with your reading of the poem.

Why is it that the poets tell
So little of the sense of smell?
These are the odors I love well:

The smell of coffee freshly ground;
Or rich plum pudding, holly-crowned;   5
Or onions fried and deeply browned.

The fragrance of a fumy pipe;
The smell of apples, newly ripe;
And printer's ink on leaden type.

Woods by moonlight in September   10
Breathe most sweet; and I remember
Many a smoky campfire ember.

Camphor, turpentine, and tea,
The balsam of a Christmas tree,
These are whiffs of gramarye . . .   15
A ship smells best of all to me!

15. *gramarye:* magic, enchantment

How many of these sensuous pleasures do you share with Mr.
Morley? In what way has this poem helped you to extend vicariously
your sense impressions?

The stanza form in which this poem (except the last stanza) is
written is called a *tercet,* a three-line stanza. In this poem, what are
the meter and the rime scheme?

You have some notion of what it means to be without the sense of
sight, or the sense of hearing. What do you think it would be like to
be deprived of the sense of smell?

A SALAD

Sydney Smith

This poem is actually a recipe, which you may like to try.
The first paragraph tells you how to prepare the sauce (condiment)
that dresses the greens; the second applauds the final result.

To make this condiment, your poet begs
The pounded yellow of two hard-boiled eggs;
Two boiled potatoes, passed through kitchen sieve,
Smoothness and softness to the salad give;
Let onion atoms lurk within the bowl,   5
And, half-suspected, animate the whole.
Of mordant mustard add a single spoon,
Distrust the condiment that bites so soon;
But deem it not, thou man of herbs, a fault,
To add a double quantity of salt;   10

Four times the spoon with oil from Lucca drown,
And twice with vinegar procured from town;
And lastly, o'er the flavored compound toss
A magic soupçon of anchovy sauce.

Oh, green and glorious! Oh, herbaceous treat!   15
'Twould tempt the dying anchorite to eat:
Back to the world he'd turn his fleeting soul,
And plunge his fingers in the salad-bowl!
Serenely full, the epicure would say,
Fate cannot harm me, I have dined today.   20

7. *mordant:* biting
11. *oil from Lucca:* olive oil from Italy
14. *soupçon:* a very small portion
16. *anchorite:* religious recluse

If the salad in your imagination tasted so delicious that you were impelled to make the salad, compare your imaginative taste with the real.

The exaggeration in the second part is used for what effect?

What is the metrical pattern in which this poem is written? (This pattern is particularly appropriate to this kind of poetry, which is known as *didactic.**)

THE SHELL

James Stephens

At some time in your life you may have held a sea shell up to your ear and listened. See if this poem does not add a new dimension to that experience. Also, you will find in it a most interesting blending of appeals to the senses of sound and of sight. The last line with its unliquid sounds very neatly brings you back to the world of everyday.

And then I pressed the shell
Close to my ear
And listened well,
And straightway like a bell
Came low and clear   5

* *Didactic poems* are poems written to instruct or teach a lesson, and by some persons are not considered to be true lyrics.

71

The slow, sad murmur of the distant seas,
Whipped by an icy breeze
Upon a shore
Wind-swept and desolate.
It was a sunless strand that never bore   10
The footprint of a man,
Nor felt the weight
Since time began
Of any human quality or stir
Save what the dreary winds and waves incur.   15
And in the hush of waters was the sound
Of pebbles rolling round,
Forever rolling with a hollow sound.
And bubbling sea-weeds as the waters go
Swish to and fro   20
Their long, cold tentacles of slimy gray.
There was no day,
Nor ever came a night
Setting the stars alight
To wonder at the moon: 25
Was twilight only and the frightened croon,
Smitten to whimpers, of the dreary wind
And waves that journeyed blind—
And then I loosed my ear . . . O, it was sweet
To hear a cart go jolting down the street.   30

How much of the imagery in this poem is new to your sense experiences? What lines do you especially enjoy? Why?

In order to catch the cadence of the music in words, read this poem aloud. It is written in an unusual combination of free verse and rime.

What emotional reaction, if any, did you have from this oral reading?

IN THE GARDEN OF THE LORD
Helen Keller

This poem by the famous Helen Keller points out joyously how a blind person can "see" the beauty around and inside himself. Note that although imagery often recreates impressions of the sense of sight, here there are very definite sense impressions of the senses of smell and touch.

> The word of God came unto me,
> Sitting alone among the multitudes;
> And my blind eyes were touched with light,
> And there was laid upon my lips a flame of fire.

> I laugh and shout, for life is good,   5
> Though my feet are set in silent ways.
> In merry mood I leave the crowd
> To walk in my garden. Ever as I walk
> I gather fruits and flowers in my hands.
> And with joyful heart I bless the sun   10
> That kindles all the place with radiant life.

> I run with playful winds that blow the scent
> Of rose and jessamine in eddying whirls.
> At last I come where tall lilies grow,
> Lifting their faces like white saints to God.   15
> While the lilies pray, I kneel upon the ground;
> I have strayed into the holy temple of the Lord.

Did you feel a bit ashamed, as I do whenever I read this poem, that you get such limited joy from your senses compared to the sensuous ecstasy Helen Keller, though deaf and blind, achieves? I hope, through poetry, you, too, will come to a fine and full life of the senses.

Sense Impressions Plus

By sharpening the antennae of your senses and making you a connoisseur of sights, sounds, feels, smells, and tastes, the lyric poet adds greatly to your sensuous pleasure. But most lyric poets give you more than pleasant mental images. They view the world about them not only with their senses but also with their minds and hearts. They try to transfer to you not only their sense images but also their thoughts and emotions concerning these objects in the world of sense experiences. Their intent is to show you the significance, the beauty, the glory of these things and make you *feel* toward them as they feel. (Remember the poet's advice in "Barter"?) For example, an image that has long existed in my mind is one of a circular bed of white geraniums. The bed was in the center of a long wide walk that led to a pavilion in a public park. The diameter of the bed was probably five feet. Weeds and wild grass did not intrude. Around that image or contained in it is a white joy of all summer long seeing that bed of white geraniums glorious under the hot midwestern sun! If, by words, I could so well transfer to you this sense impression that you not only saw the image but felt some of my feeling accompanying it, I would be accomplishing what the lyric poet desires: the happy marriage of image and emotion.

SUNRISE

Lizette Woodworth Reese

The poet wants to share with you the thrill she got from a particular sunrise. Visualize the details and be alert for words that are conveyers of emotion.

The east is yellow as a daffodil.
Three steeples—three stark swarthy arms—are thrust
Up from the town. The gnarled poplars thrill
Down the long street in some keen salty gust—
Straight from the sea and all the sailing ships— [Parenthetical.] 5
Turn white, black, white again, with noises sweet [Refers to the
And swift. Back to the night the last star slips.   poplars.]
High up the air is motionless, a sheet
Of light. The east grows yellower apace,
And trembles: then, once more, and suddenly,   10
The salt wind blows, and in that moment's space
Flame roofs, and poplar-tops, and steeples three; [*Flame* is the verb.]
From out the mist that wraps the river-ways,
The little boats, like torches, start ablaze.

The sunrise described occurs in what kind of place? Have you had a similar experience? What emotion did the poem arouse in you? What words help to convey emotion?
To what extent does the poem conform to the requirements of a sonnet?
Find examples of alliteration.

DAWN

William Carlos Williams

The author, in this lyric, has caught in words a small miracle in nature—the songs of birds bringing in the dawn and sunrise. Put yourself in the situation, go along with the poet, see if he does not awaken you to the glory of the everyday occurrence of dawn.

Ecstatic bird songs pound
the hollow vastness of the sky
with metallic clinkings—   [The sharp notes of certain birds.]
beating color up into it   [The color of dawn which
at a far edge,—beating it, beating it   precedes the sunrise.]
                                          [The *it* consistently refers   5
with rising, triumphant ardor,—   to the sky.]
stirring it into warmth,
quickening in it a spreading change,—
bursting wildly against it as   [The songs burst.]
dividing the horizon, a heavy sun   [The sun divides the horizon.]   10
lifts himself—is lifted—
bit by bit above the edge
of things,—runs free at last
out into the open—! lumbering
glorified in full release upward—   15
                songs cease.

Compare this poem with the preceding one by Lizette Woodworth Reese. Which of the poems is to you the more emotionally stirring? Why?

This poem is worth a little study in order to increase your understanding of free verse. Notice the control used. Notice how each phrase, each line adds to the total effect. In your opinion what effect is obtained by the use of the dashes?

RADAR

A. M. Sullivan

Science and poetry join company in this poem. You are familiar with radar and its connection with the warning system established all over the country. Perched atop buildings, mountains, or out on sandy beaches are the radar antennae, the magical big "ears," listening, watching. (The poet has dispensed with the usual punctuation conventions, but I hope this practice will not hamper your reading.)

Tongues with the speed of light
Challenge all things in flight
And search the good and evil in the dark

And when the echo's heard   [Effective image. Note
Ears grip the electric word   author's technical   5
And measure the hidden journey of a spark   understanding.]

And the ear becomes an eye
Over the sea and high   [Mentally put a period
                                      after *climb*.]
As falcons climb and man shall stand aware [Read on. No period here.]

Of approaching foe or friend   10
Beyond the horizon's bend
And in the darkness he shall meet them there.

What emotion pervades the poem?
Some knowledgeable student should explain the principle of radar and show how the author reveals in the poem an awareness of that principle.
Compare the meter and rime of these tercets with those in "Smells" on page 69.

CAT'S EYE
Paul Engle

The situation presented in this poem is something like this: the physical geography of the world has gone awry and the world is about to explode and you are the last man alive. Under such conditions you are asked what one thing you would like to see. Be prepared for some long sentences and run-on lines. The imagery is most powerful. I don't believe you will have trouble grasping the main thought, which brims with glory. Be sure to read the poem aloud!

If suddenly blackness crawled   [Note the effective verbs.]
Over the world and the sun hurtled down
The vast and verge of space until it glowed   [*Vast* and *verge* (edge)
No bigger than a cat's eye in the night,   are nouns.]
And wind beat the bruised face of the earth with awful   5

76

Tornado-clubbing fists, and all the waters
Rose in a leaping body to the heavens   [Powerful sight
Tidally challenging the moon, and then   and sound
With foaming, gibbering mouth went howling over imagery.]
The shuddering plains and ocean bottoms: 10
                              If stars
Splattered and dashed the sky, and the moon wallowed
Dark without the sun, and I were the last
Man moving through the streets of towns the tiny
Pale hands of men had fashioned, and out of the shouting   15
Air and split space and trembling earth a voice
Asked softly what one thing I wished to see
Before the universe grew tense and cracked
To the core, and burst beyond the farthest gaunt
Galaxies of heaven, I would plead   20
That through the shadow there would loom the friendly
White magnificence of a human face.

I WANDERED LONELY AS A CLOUD
William Wordsworth

Have you ever had the experience of suddenly becoming
aware of an object of beauty? Read about such an incident, and see
if the poet passes on to you some of his joy in discovering the daffodils.
So impressive was that emotional experience that it lived forever in
the poet's mind. Recall upon recall brought pleasure and continued
delight. This poem makes very clear the meaning and value of storing
up sense impressions.

I wandered lonely as a cloud
That floats on high o'er vales and hills,
When all at once I saw a crowd,
A host, of golden daffodils;
Beside the lake, beneath the trees,   5
Fluttering and dancing in the breeze.

Continuous as the stars that shine
And twinkle on the milky way,
They stretched in never-ending line

Along the margin of a bay:
Ten thousand saw I at a glance,
Tossing their heads in sprightly dance.

The waves beside them danced; but they
Out-did the sparkling waves in glee:
A poet could not but be gay,   [The scene has affected 15
In such a jocund company: the poet's mood.]
I gazed—and gazed—but little thought
What wealth the show to me had brought:

                                                [Time lapse.]
For oft, when on my couch I lie   [The wealth
In vacant or in pensive mood,   of the experience 20
They flash upon that inward eye   is realized.]
Which is the bliss of solitude;
And then my heart with pleasure fills,
And dances with the daffodils.

What vivid and time-tested sense impressions of your own do you recall with real pleasure? Try to get one of these experiences expressed by means of imagery.

Figures of Speech (Comparisons)

Imagery, as you have been discovering in the preceding pages, is a means by which sensuous experiences are shared. Through images-in-words the poet transfers his sense impressions from his mind to yours. However, it is sometimes difficult to transmit certain sense impressions. To tell you how salt tastes or lilacs smell is very hard. I probably just have to ask you to taste salt or to smell a lilac. But in other instances I can assist the transfer of the same impression by using a familiar image to help you create another image, a new, unfamiliar one. I say to you that a nectarine tastes partly like a peach and partly like an apricot. I have made a comparison. I have operated on the basis that you know how a peach and an apricot taste, and that your mind is able to transfer details from the familiar tastes to the taste image I want you to develop in your mind. Let's take another example.

I want you to see the very blushing face of a much embarrassed mother. To help you see as I see, I say that her face is as red as a beet. I have used the familiar image, the color of the beet, to make sure that you sense the other image, the deeply blushing face. Sometimes the comparison is implied rather than stated. When the poet Longfellow called the stars the forget-me-nots of the angels, he was using an implied comparison to make you see the stars as he saw them, both sensuously and emotionally.

Such comparisons, stated or implied, are called figures of speech (simile, metaphor, personification, and symbol).*

Simile

A *simile* is a comparison directly expressing that one thing is like another. The joining words are *like, as,* and *than.*

THE FLY
Walter de la Mare

This little poem consists almost entirely of similes. Look for the words *like* and *as.* Through the figures of speech the poet helps us to see imaginatively the fly's world. (Notice that all the objects selected—the rosebud, the thorn, the dewdrop, etc.—are common to the fly's experience.)

> How large unto the tiny fly
> Must little things appear!—
> A rosebud like a feather bed,
> Its prickle like a spear;
>
> A dew-drop like a looking glass,   5
> A hair like golden wire;
> The smallest grain of mustard-seed
> As fierce as coals of fire;

---

* *Figures of speech,* called *tropes,* are not limited to comparisons, as you will learn if you continue your study of imagery beyond this elementary volume. Also, in your reading in other books you may discover that *metaphor* (not *a* metaphor) is used to include all figures of speech which are comparisons. To speak *metaphorically* means to speak not literally, but *figuratively.*

A loaf of bread, a lofty hill;
A wasp, a cruel leopard;   10
And specks of salt as bright to see
As lambkins to a shepherd.

Which of the images in the poet's conception of the fly's mind has
the poet been able to transfer to your mind? Which of the similes do
you think are especially effective? Why?

Explain whether or not the stanza pattern conforms to that of the
common measure.

Metaphor

Whereas a simile is an *expressed* comparison, a *metaphor* is an
implied comparison which does not use a connecting word such
as *like* or *as*.

DREAMS

Langston Hughes

In this poem each stanza contains a metaphor. Take note how
much each figure of speech says. It is as if the poet had said, "To
make you realize how I feel about life without dreams is pretty hard.
But . . . perhaps some time or other you have seen a broken-winged
bird and a barren field covered with snow. And when you recall these
sights, the emotions which well up in you are the same as my emo-
tions when I see the barrenness of the lives of human beings in whom
all dreams are dead. Now do you understand?"

Hold fast to dreams
For if dreams die
Life is a broken-winged bird
That can not fly.

Hold fast to dreams   5
For when dreams go
Life is a barren field
Frozen with snow.

If you have read alertly, you will have perceived just why life has been likened to a certain kind of bird, and a certain kind of field. Writing a prose statement of the full meaning conveyed by each metaphor is an excellent way to grasp how much such a figure of speech can say. I suggest you do this.

This poem illustrates the fact that "figures of speech" are not limited to comparisons of literal sensuous images, but may be used to clarify abstract ideas or complex emotions. At this point you might read again "A Red, Red Rose," page 26.

Personification

Personification is a kind of metaphor which treats an abstraction or object (inanimate) as if it were a person (animate). If to such abstractions as honesty, simplicity, love, or to inanimate objects like earth, sun, rock, human traits are assigned, these abstractions, or these objects, have become *personified*.

FRAGMENT FROM NOTHING
Elizabeth Coatsworth

The abstraction hate is deftly personified in this little poem. (The possessive pronoun *her* refers to Hate, not to Fear.)

> And Hate,
> Fear's ugliest child,
> held to her skirts
> and while she curtseyed,
> glared up like a toad.   [Simile.] 5

What particular kind of hate is personified? (It is not the wild, unleashed kind: note the curtsey!) What is the significance of calling Hate the child of Fear? Give examples of hates which have been created by fear. According to your imagination, who may be some other children of Fear?

What was your emotional response to this poem?

Try your hand at personifying some abstraction, in prose or poetry —perhaps in a couplet.

Symbol

A *symbol* is a peculiar kind of image, one which, generally because of tradition, embodies an idea or quality. For instance, I have in my mind an image of the American flag being carried past me in a parade. But the flag is more than just some red-white-and-blue cloth arranged as stars and stripes. It is a symbol of all that the United States stands for: "One nation, under God, indivisible, with liberty and justice for all." And if I write, "Hats off! The flag is passing by," I am attempting to transfer to the reader not only an image of the flag but also the *ideas* embodied but not stated in that image.

See if you do not recognize at least a few of the following traditional symbols *and* their embodied notions. There are the seasons of the year:

> spring —birth, rebirth, childhood
> summer—growth, young manhood
> autumn —maturity
> winter —old age, death

Others that have long enriched literature are:

> river; a climb—life, man's journey through life
> water   —a renewal, a rebirth
> fire   —a consuming love or hate, zeal
> light   —goodness, God
> darkness   —evil, Satan, ignorance

Poets frequently use such *symbols,* and you as an educated reader of such specialized imagery must not miss the *ideas* embodied in the images. Let us fortify this explanation by carefully reading a poem in which the author has made a quite obvious use of symbols.

THE LONG HILL

Sara Teasdale

In this poem you visualize a hill, a climb up the hill, and a descent therefrom, but the poet is really talking not about a hill but about life. Read the poem through once to get an overall notion. Read it a second time, especially noticing the marginal aids.

I must have passed the crest
    a while ago
And now I am going down—
Strange to have crossed the
    crest and not to know,
    But the brambles were al-
    ways catching the hem of
    my gown.

[The person has passed the high point, or maturity, of life without being aware that it was reached.]

All the morning I thought how
    proud I should be
To stand there straight as a
    queen,
Wrapped in the wind and the
    sun with the world under
    me—
    But the air was dull, there
    was little I could have seen.

[In youth the person looked forward to maturity, enjoying the anticipated elation.] 5

[At length recognizing that the peak has been reached, and passed, the person is disillusioned. Life is pretty ordinary and dull.]

It was nearly level along the
    beaten track
And the brambles caught in
    my gown—
But it's no use now to think of
    turning back,
    The rest of the way will be
    only going down.

[Life cannot be lived over. The person is resigned to a decline. 10 Life was consumed by pettinesses and small cares.]

Sometimes a poet creates symbols of his own, not generally accepted by tradition. In "The Long Hill" the poet made use of one:

But the brambles were always catching the hem of my gown. . . .

The person's journey through life (the climb up the hill, etc.) was hindered and halted by having to take care of life's petty little distractions (the idea that *brambles* embodies to me).

    What is your reaction to the idea expressed in the last two lines of the poem? What is your interpretation of the word *long* in the title?

    What term best describes the mood of this poem?

What variations in stanzaic pattern do you find in the second and third stanzas from that established in the first one?

Three Poems: A Summing Up

As a climax to your study of imagery, I hope that each of these three poems will provide you with a pleasurable sensuous and emotional experience. Be alert to appeals to all of the five senses. Use your imagination so that you will get genuine enjoyment from the figurative language.

CLEAN CURTAINS
Carl Sandburg

In this poem, which contains symbols, the poet is commenting upon a situation he probably observed during his own stay in Chicago. The conflict between two ways of life is represented by the symbols of the curtains versus the dust and trucks.

New neighbors came to the corner house [Note the alliterations.]
    at Congress and Green Streets.

The look of their clean white curtains was [Symbol introduced.]
    the same as the rim of a nun's bonnet. [Simile.]

One way was an oyster-pail factory, one
    way they made candy, one way paper
    boxes, strawboard cartons.

The warehouse trucks shook the dust of [Effective repetition.
    the ways loose and the wheels Symbol value of
    whirled dust—there was dust of hoof *dust* and *trucks*.]
    and wagon wheel and rubber tire—
    dust of police and fire wagons—dust
    of the winds that circled at midnight
    and noon listening to no prayers.

"O mother, I know the heart of you," I
    sang passing the rim of a nun's bon- [Metaphor.]
    net—O white curtains—and people

84

clean as the prayers of Jesus here in   [Simile.]
the faded ramshackle at Congress
and Green.

Dust and the thundering trucks won—the   [Symbols.]
barrages of the street wheels and the
lawless wind took their way—was it
five weeks or six the little mother, the
new neighbors, battled and then took
away the white prayers in the win-   [Symbol.]
dows?

What senses are appealed to? What feeling prevails after you have
read the poem? Did you find any phrase that dates the poem?
What progression from division to division did you observe? Would
you call these divisions stanzas? Why not?

CRYSTAL MOMENT

Robert P. Tristram Coffin

Some lyric poems are concerned with incidents. When we
read them, we think of narration. But then we realize that the poet is
not really interested in telling a story. Rather, he has been moved to
ponder over the meaning of the incident. These little happenings can
be so intensely experienced that, even from childhood, we remember
them for life.

Once or twice this side of death
Things can make one hold his breath.

From my boyhood I remember
A crystal moment of September.

A wooded island rang with sounds   5
Of church bells in the throats of hounds.

A buck leaped out and took the tide
With jewels flowing past each side.

With his high head like a tree
He swam within a yard of me.   10

I saw the golden drop of light
In his eyes turned dark with fright.

I saw the forest's holiness
On him like a fierce caress.

Fear made him lovely past belief,   15
My heart was trembling like a leaf.   [Simile most appropriate
                                        to the setting.]
He leaned toward the land and life
With need upon him like a knife.

In his wake the hot hounds churned,
They stretched their muzzles out and
    yearned.   20

They bayed no more, but swam and
    throbbed,
Hunger drove them till they sobbed.

Pursued, pursuers reached the shore   [The report of the
And vanished. I saw nothing more.   incident ends.]

So they passed, a pageant such   25
As only gods could witness much,   [Read on, no period.]

Life and death upon one tether
And running beautiful together.

What indirect comment does the poem make on hunting? What is
your interpretation of the last four lines? How do you relate the title
and its meaning to the poem?

Based on your own performance, what advice can you give to the
person who wants to read the poem aloud effectively?

THE FISH

Elizabeth Bishop

The next time you go fishing take a very, very good look at
the fish you catch. Or, through the poet's remarkable power of obser-
vation, look right now at the fish you have just caught. Relish the
unusually striking and fresh similes. See if the emotion evoked by

the imagery helps you to understand why, in the end, you do what
you do.

I caught a tremendous fish
and held him beside the boat
half out of water, with my hook
fast in a corner of his mouth.
He didn't fight. 5
He hadn't fought at all.
He hung a grunting weight,
battered and venerable
and homely. Here and there
his brown skin hung in strips 10
like ancient wallpaper,
and its pattern of darker brown
was like wallpaper:
shapes like full-blown roses
stained and lost through age. 15
He was speckled with barnacles,
fine rosettes of lime,
and infested
with tiny white sea-lice,
and underneath two or three 20
rags of green weed hung down.
While his gills were breathing in
the terrible oxygen
—the frightening gills
fresh and crisp with blood, 25
that can cut so badly—
I thought of the coarse white flesh
packed in like feathers,
the big bones and the little bones,
the dramatic reds and blacks 30
of his shiny entrails,
and the pink swim-bladder
like a big peony.
I looked into his eyes
which were far larger than mine 35
but shallower, and yellowed,

the irises backed and packed
with tarnished tinfoil
seen through the lenses
of old scratched isinglass.   40
They shifted a little, but not
to return my stare.
—It was more like the tipping
of an object toward the light.
I admired his sullen face,   45
the mechanism of his jaw,
and then I saw
that from his lower lip
—if you could call it a lip—
grim, wet, and weaponlike,   50
hung five old pieces of fish-line,
or four and a wire leader
with the swivel still attached,
with all their five big hooks
grown firmly in his mouth.   55
A green line, frayed at the end
where he broke it, two heavier lines,
and a fine black thread
still crimped from the strain and snap
when it broke and he got away.   60
Like medals with their ribbons
frayed and wavering,
a five-haired beard of wisdom
trailing from his aching jaw.
I stared and stared   65
and victory filled up
the little rented boat,
from the pool of bilge
where oil had spread a rainbow
around the rusted engine   70
to the bailer rusted orange,
the sun-cracked thwarts,
the oarlocks on their strings,
the gunnels—until everything

was rainbow, rainbow, rainbow!
And I let the fish go.

What progression is made in the poem?

Of what, in the end, did you feel the fish became a symbol?

In which of the wonderful similes did you find the most pleasure?

In what way did this poem extend your sensuous experiences?

Try writing a straightforward nonfigurative description of a fish (or of some other creature, one that you really know from experience). Then write a second description in which you consciously employ figures of speech. Make the figures of speech serve your end: to make the object come alive for the reader.

The Vision of the Ideal

LYRIC VERSE can give you pleasure through its power to hold before you the vision of the ideal.

Before you is life and the vision of the ideal, the art of living the good life. You realize that the world is far from perfect and that there is room for considerable improvement; and with something of a crusader's determination, your mind challenges the demons of sham and shame. The affirmations and questionings that you debate with yourself in the privacy of your soul, they, too, are a part of living the good life nobly. As you have questioned, so have the poets: Is justice dead? What can I do to lessen "man's inhumanity to man"? What am I here for? What is life all about? What is death? And beyond, what?

You can find in lyric verse answers to many such troubling questions. Out of the feelings and aspirations, out of the admonitions and prayers that are given tongue in lyric verse can come a genuine inspiration, from the simple, direct sermon in rime to the most sublime and profound meditation. Lyric verse has in it the power to help you make your mind supple, your spirit imaginative, and your heart compassionate.

Let poetry exert its influence in your life and inspire you to live life more abundantly. And in lyric verse especially, may you find the music that heals the common cares and the spiritual muscle that brings victory over the baser greeds and twisted truths that flesh is heir to. There may you find enthusiasm to welcome the future, to treasure the present, to respect the past— above all, to reverence the Divine in humble man at his highest stature and unselfish best.

TO JAMES

Frank Horne

Those of you who have been out for track will especially enjoy this bit of advice in verse. I have not found a boy or girl who did not like this poem.

Do you remember
How you won
That last race . . . ?
How you flung your body
At the start . . .   5
How your spikes
Ripped the cinders
In the stretch . . .
How you catapulted
Through the tape . . .   10
Do you remember . . . ?
Don't you think
I lurched with you
Out of those starting holes . . . ?
Don't you think   15
My sinews tightened
At those first
Few strides . . .
And when you flew into the stretch
Was not all my thrill   20
Of a thousand races
In your blood?
At your final drive
Through the finish line
Did not my shout   25
Tell of the
Triumphant ecstasy
Of victory . . . ?
Live
As I have taught you   30

To run, Boy—
It's a short dash.
Dig your starting holes
Deep and firm.
Lurch out of them   35
Into the straightaway
With all the power
That is in you
Look straight ahead
To the finish line   40
Think only of the goal
Run straight
Run high
Run hard
Save nothing   45
And finish
With an ecstatic burst
That carries you
Hurtling
Through the tape   50
To victory . . .

In what way does this poem illuminate the relationship between a father and a son? (Or is it a coach and an athlete?)

How is life like, and not like, a race? Explain whether or not the poet has made use of a traditional symbol.

To what senses did the poem appeal? What emotion did the poem stir within you?

MOTHER TO SON

Langston Hughes

For some persons life has been pretty tough sledding. It is a real inspiration to see that some individuals among these persons not only hold before themselves the vision of the ideal but also make a real effort to pass it on to their sons and daughters. The mother speaks in a dialectal language characteristic of her.

Well, son, I'll tell you:
Life for me ain't been no crystal stair.

It's had tacks in it,
And splinters,
And boards torn up,   5
And places with no carpet on the floor—

But all the time
I'se been a-climbin' on,
And reachin' landin's,
And turnin' corners   10
And sometimes goin' in the dark
When there ain't no light.

So, boy, don't you turn back.
Don't you set down on the steps
'Cause you find it's kinder hard.   15
Don't you fall now—
For I'se still goin', honey,
I'se still climbin'
And life for me ain't been no crystal stair.

What kind of person is the mother? Explain whether or not the imagery she uses is consistent with her character and the situation.

In both "To James" and "Mother to Son" a parent's advice to a son is influenced by the parent's own experience. How, and when, does this experience have value? Which poem did you find of the greater value to you? Why?

A FAREWELL

Charles Kingsley

In this poem a parting of two people motivates some kindly advice, which, if taken to heart and cherished, can lead on to happiness.

My fairest child, I have no song to give you;
    No lark could pipe to skies so dull and gray;
Yet, ere we part, one lesson I can leave you
    For every day.

Be good, sweet maid, and let who will be clever;   5
    Do noble things, not dream them, all day long:

And so make life, death, and that vast forever
One grand, sweet song.

To whom and under what circumstances might you quote this poem?

To what extent do you agree, or disagree, with the implication about goodness and cleverness that the poet makes in line 5?

By what variations did the author keep the rhythm from becoming monotonous?

OUTWITTED

Edwin Markham

This quatrain is a little lesson in what it takes to love your neighbor as yourself.

He drew a circle that shut me out—
Heretic, rebel, a thing to flout,
But Love and I had the wit to win:
We drew a circle that took him in!

What is the unexpressed object of *win* in line three? Give examples from your own experience or observation of persons who "won" by drawing a large enough circle.

IT IS NOT GROWING LIKE A TREE

Ben Jonson

In this poem, through imagery drawn from plant life, Jonson reminds us that a full and beautiful life is not measured necessarily by size or age. Because we do not know that we shall live to forty, sixty, or seventy-five, we must live richly and in beauty and harmony as we go along from day to day.

It is not growing like a tree
In bulk, doth make man better be;
Or standing long an oak, three hundred year,
To fall a log at last, dry, bald, and sere;
A lily of a day   5
Is fairer far in May,

Although it fall and die that night,
It was the plant and flower of light.
In small proportions we just beauties see;
And in short measures, life may perfect be.   10

What would be your reaction to the reading of this poem at the
funeral of a young person? This poem is especially beneficial to what
kind of person?
A critic has called this poem "clean cut and shapely." What do you
think he meant?

IF—

Rudyard Kipling

Kipling, in this very famous poem, writes his definition of
what it means when we say, "Be a man." So well-known has his poem
become that I fear many people know it and about it but have never
stopped to digest the "if's" that are the substance of the definition.
Do not rush through this example of a thought expressed in verse.

If you can keep your head when all about you
    Are losing theirs and blaming it on you;
If you can trust yourself when all men doubt you,
    But make allowance for their doubting too;
If you can wait and not be tired by waiting,   5
Or, being lied about, don't deal in lies,
Or, being hated, don't give way to hating,
    And yet don't look too good, nor talk too wise;

If you can dream—and not make dreams your master;
    If you can think—and not make thoughts your aim;   10
If you can meet with triumph and disaster
    And treat those two impostors just the same;
If you can bear to hear the truth you've spoken
    Twisted by knaves to make a trap for fools,
Or watch the things you gave your life to broken,   15
    And stoop and build 'em up with wornout tools;

If you can make one heap of all your winnings
    And risk it on one turn of pitch-and-toss,

And lose, and start again at your beginnings
 And never breathe a word about your loss;   20
If you can force your heart and nerve and sinew
 To serve your turn long after they are gone,
And so hold on when there is nothing in you
 Except the Will which says to them: "Hold on";

If you can talk with crowds and keep your virtue,   25
 Or walk with kings—nor lose the common touch;
If neither foes nor loving friends can hurt you;
 If all men count with you, but none too much;
If you can fill the unforgiving minute
 With sixty seconds' worth of distance run—   30
Yours is the Earth and everything that's in it,
 And—which is more—you'll be a Man, my son!

What characteristics of the ideal man are enumerated in this poem?
How many of these have been put to test in your own experiences?
Are there any "if's" with which you are in disagreement?

What is the prevailing meter? What variations are used? Find examples of effective alliteration.

Look up, in Shakespeare's *Hamlet*, Polonius's advice to his son
Laertes. Compare "If—" with the passage.

GOD, GIVE US MEN!

Josiah Gilbert Holland

Here is a poem that is a standard bearer for the art of living
the good life. See if it does not thrill you to read a poem in which the
author speaks his mind for the virtues that make this world a better
place in which to live.

God, give us men! A time like this demands
Strong minds, great hearts, true faith and ready hands;
 Men whom the lust of office does not kill;
Men whom the spoils of office cannot buy;
 Men who possess opinions and a will;   5
Men who have honor; men who will not lie;
Men who can stand before a demagogue

And damn his treacherous flatteries without winking!
Tall men, sun-crowned, who live above the fog
  In public duty and in private thinking;   10
For while the rabble, with their thumb-worn creeds,
Their large professions and their little deeds,
Mingle in selfish strife, lo! Freedom weeps,
Wrong rules the land and waiting Justice sleeps.

Memorize this poem. It may be useful to you some day.
What departures from the traditional sonnet forms do you find?
Find examples of personification.

THE CHAMBERED NAUTILUS
Oliver Wendell Holmes

Great lessons from little things! Have you ever stopped to
contemplate and conjecture about the arrowhead discovered in the
field, or the curious rock fetched home, or the shell picked up on
the beach? Your curiosity is aroused; you see the object in relation
to larger things and—flash—there comes that insight of meaningful-
ness. May Holmes's mental exaltation, stated precisely and musically,
be transferred to you.

In the course of its life the nautilus inhabits successively a series
of enlarging compartments within its shell that form a widening spiral.

The poem is worth the careful reading it demands. Note the pro-
gression: stanzas one through three picture the nautilus, stanza four
offers a thanksgiving, and five states the lesson learned from the object.

This is the ship of pearl, which, poets feign,
  Sails the unshadowed main,—
  The venturous bark that flings
On the sweet summer wind its purpled wings
In gulfs enchanted, where the Siren sings,   5
  And coral reefs lie bare,
Where the cold sea-maids rise to sun their streaming hair.

Its webs of living gauze no more unfurl;
  Wrecked is the ship of pearl!
  And every chambered cell,   10

Where its dim dreaming life was wont to dwell,
As the frail tenant shaped his growing shell,
   Before thee lies revealed,—
Its irised ceiling rent, its sunless crypt unsealed!

Year after year beheld the silent toil   15
   That spread his lustrous coil;
   Still, as the spiral grew,
He left the past year's dwelling for the new,
Stole with soft step its shining archway through,
   Built up its idle door,   20
Stretched in his last-found home, and knew the old no more.

Thanks for the heavenly message brought by thee,
   Child of the wandering sea,
   Cast from her lap, forlorn!
From thy dead lips a clearer note is born   25
Than ever Triton blew from wreathèd horn!
   While on mine ear it rings,
Through the deep caves of thought I hear a voice that sings:—

Build thee more stately mansions, O my soul,
   As the swift seasons roll!   30
   Leave thy low-vaulted past!
Let each new temple, nobler than the last,
Shut thee from heaven with a dome more vast,
   Till thou at length art free,
Leaving thine outgrown shell by life's unresting sea!   35

5. *Siren:* sea nymph whose song enticed seamen to their deaths
14. *irised:* rainbow-colored
26. *Triton:* sea god, half-man and half-fish, whose horn was a conch shell

In what way did the reading of this poem make you feel better inside yourself?

Point out examples of especially rich imagery. What extra imaginative touches has the poet added to the setting of the nautilus's home?

What are the characteristics of the stanzaic pattern?

The use of some simple subject as a basis for a lesson was common among our famous New England poets of the nineteenth century. What other such poems do you know? They are an important part of our American literary heritage.

LEISURE

William H. Davies

Do you think it is wise to become so wrapped up with pursuits, often vain or material ones, that you lose sight of the beauty about you—in people, places, and things? Remember to keep the senses alert and new riches will be forthcoming—and free.

What is this life, if, full of care,
We have no time to stand and stare,

No time to stand beneath the boughs
And stare as long as sheep or cows.

No time to see, when woods we pass,   5
Where squirrels hide their nuts in grass.

No time to see, in broad daylight,
Streams full of stars, like skies at night.

No time to turn at Beauty's glance,
And watch her feet, how they can dance.   10

No time to wait till her mouth can
Enrich that smile her eyes began.

A poor life this if, full of care,
We have no time to stand and stare.

Write an essay expressing your opinion on the valuable use of leisure, or develop your notion about the abuse of leisure in these times.

Find examples of figures of speech.

PRELIMINARY POEM FOR A MODERN CITY

Harry Kemp

During the very years that you have been growing up, there has been a great deal of building, of tearing down, and of building anew: homes, office buildings, apartment buildings, schools, churches. Some of you have probably lamented the loss of old beautiful structures; others of you have found it exciting to see the new replace the old. Read how a poet has reacted to this cycle of tearing down and constructing again.

The wreckers heave, and lift, and split, on twenty sites, in town;
They make the wood and plaster fly by ripping buildings down;
But here is one who'll never stand in sentimental tears
While the future, looking onward, checks the past for its arrears.
Mansions of grace and stately port that have outseen their day 5
Are not the only ones to go; vile hulks of dark decay
Will crawl no more with abjectness, but in their stead shall rise
Height upon height of lusty youth whose tops shall be the skies!
The honest, happy wreckers, when they've razed the area clean,
Will pack their kits and throng away as if they had not been, 10
And the structural ironworkers, laying floor on floor, will come,
And the riveter's close-pressed hammer will throb, martial, like a
    drum!
Ten thousand windows for the dawn! ten thousand for the fire
Of evening! Be a place for men wherein they may aspire.
O Skyward-Builded City, heap your summits
    high, and free   [*Free* is a verb.] 15
The hearts of men to greater heights of life's reality!

Look up the various meanings of *sentiment* and *sentimentality*. What is the meaning, in line 3, of the phrase *sentimental tears?*

From your own experience think of examples of structures you hated to see torn down and of others you gladly let be destroyed. How do these feelings relate to your aspirations? To your attitude toward the past, present, and future?

How do the meter and the rime scheme differ from that in the poem "Leisure" on page 99?

FOR A' THAT AND A' THAT
Robert Burns

In this poem, Robert Burns, that self-educated Scottish farmer, speaks with determined conviction that eventually common man's common sense and pride in man's worth will lead to universal brotherhood—an ideal that man has held throughout the ages.

Is there, for honest poverty,
That hangs his head, and a' that;
The coward-slave, we pass him by,
We dare be poor for a' that!
For a' that, and a' that,   5
Our toils obscure, and a' that,
The rank is but the guinea's stamp,
The man's the gowd for a' that.

What though on hamely fare we dine,
Wear hoddin grey, and a' that;   10
Gie fools their silks, and knaves their wine,
A man's a man for a' that:
For a' that, and a' that,
Their tinsel show, and a' that;
The honest man, though e'er sae poor,   15
Is king o' men for a' that.

Ye see yon birkie, ca'd a lord,
Wha struts, and stares, and a' that;
Though hundreds worship at his word,
He's but a coof for a' that: 20
For a' that, and a' that,
His ribband, star, and a' that,
The man of independent mind,
He looks and laughs at a' that.

A prince can mak a belted knight,   25
A marquis, duke, and a' that;
But an honest man's aboon his might,
Guid faith, he maunna fa' that!
For a' that, and a' that,
Their dignities, and a' that,   30
The pith o' sense and pride o' worth,
Are higher ranks than a' that.

Then let us pray that come it may,
As come it will for a' that,
That sense and worth, o'er a' the earth,   35

May bear the gree, and a' that.
For a' that, and a' that,
It's comin' yet for a' that,
That man to man, the warld o'er,
Shall brothers be for a' that.   40

7. *guinea:* a British coin
8. *gowd:* gold
10. *hoddin grey:* coarse, cheap cloth
17. *birkie:* fellow
20. *coof:* fool
27. *aboon:* above
28. *maunna fa':* cannot make
36. *bear the gree:* win the prize

In spite of the prophetic tone to this poem, or perhaps along with it, what personal prejudice is evident? The ambitious student might check the life of the author to discover what facts might be related to this bias.

What is the relationship between this poem and the idea of democracy?

What was your emotional reaction to the poem?

THE MAN HE KILLED

Thomas Hardy

I know of no other poem so simple and direct in its expression of one of the great ironies of war, namely that in peace time a man would welcome with human warmth the very "enemy" he kills in war.

"Had he and I but met
By some old ancient inn,
We should have sat us down to wet
Right many a nipperkin!

"But ranged as infantry,   5
And staring face to face,
I shot at him as he at me,
And killed him in his place.

"I shot him dead because—
Because he was my foe,   10

Just so: my foe of course he was;
   That's clear enough; although

"He thought he'd 'list, perhaps,
   Off-hand like—just as I;
Was out of work, had sold his traps—   15
   No other reason why.

"Yes; quaint and curious war is!
   You shoot a fellow down
You'd treat if met where any bar is,
   Or help to half-a-crown."   20

Even though the speaker of the poem killed a man, why would
you like to meet him?
   What did the poet gain by having both men enlist?
   Why is a less smooth rhythm appropriate in this poem? What is
the stanza pattern?

A Group of Prayers

Here is a group of prayers in verse. Read each one carefully.
You may not agree with everything in each of the prayers, but
they have been selected with care as being worthy of your atten-
tion and energy. Read to discover how many of these expressions
of human need you have shared in those private debates with
your soul and how many will have increased your understanding
of the deeper side of human nature.

PRAYER

Louis Untermeyer

In this first prayer the poet definitely looks upon this earthly
life as but a dream (wraith). In spite of this notion, he is very down-
to-earth about the things he asks as guides for himself.

God, though this life is but a wraith,
   Although we know not what we use,
Although we grope with little faith,
   Give me the heart to fight—and lose.

Ever insurgent let me be,   5
    Make me more daring than devout;
From sleek contentment keep me free,
    And fill me with a buoyant doubt.

Open my eyes to visions girt
    With beauty, and with wonder lit—   10
But let me always see the dirt,
    And all that spawn and die in it.

Open my ears to music; let
    Me thrill with Spring's first flutes and drums—
But never let me dare forget   15
    The bitter ballads of the slums.

From compromise and things half-done,
    Keep me, with stern and stubborn pride.
And when, at last, the fight is won,   [Do not read
    God, keep me still unsatisfied.   *dissatisfied.*] 20

What emotional attitude does the poet have toward life in general?
    To what extent do you feel that a person who sincerely made such
a prayer would make a good citizen? Why? Why would you want
such a person for a friend?
    Why is "bitter ballads of the slums" an especially appropriate
phrase?

A SERGEANT'S PRAYER

Hugh Brodie

Before going into battle, men naturally turn to prayer. Im-
agine yourself praying under such circumstances. This poem reveals
what one GI in World War II wanted from God, and it is reassuring
to read that malice and bitterness do not mar the clear vision that the
words of this prayer convey.

Almighty and all present Power,
Short is the prayer I make to Thee,
I do not ask in battle hour
For any shield to cover me.

The vast unalterable way,   5
From which the stars do not depart
May not be turned aside to stay
The bullet flying to my heart.

I ask no help to strike my foe,
I seek no petty victory here,   10
The enemy I hate, I know,
To Thee is also dear.

But this I pray, be at my side
When death is drawing through the sky.
Almighty God who also died,   15
Teach me the way that I should die.

How does this prayer harmonize with the concept of God as being
a loving God? What does the poem communicate about man's posi-
tion in the universe?

What is the meaning of line 15? Do you think this line would spoil
the poem for a non-Christian? Why?

THE PILLAR OF THE CLOUD
John Henry Newman

This prayer, humbly asking for Divine guidance, has become
one of the English-speaking world's most loved hymns, frequently
given the title "Lead, Kindly Light."

Lead, kindly Light, amid the encircling gloom,
    Lead Thou me on!
The night is dark, and I am far from home—
    Lead Thou me on!
Keep Thou my feet; I do not ask to see   5
The distant scene,—one step enough for me.

I was not ever thus, nor prayed that Thou
    Shouldst lead me on.
I loved to choose and see my path; but now
    Lead Thou me on!   10
I loved the garish day, and, spite of fears,
Pride ruled my will: remember not past years.

So long Thy power hath blessed me, sure it still
  Will lead me on,
O'er moor and fen, o'er crag and torrent, till   15
  The night is gone;
And with the morn those angel faces smile
Which I have loved long since, and lost awhile.

What is the central thought of the poem?
Point out ways in which the phrase "in rich figurative poetry" can
be applied to the poem.
What is the prevailing meter?

PRAYER OF COLUMBUS

Walt Whitman

I quote a portion of Whitman's own introduction to the poem:
"It was near the close of his indomitable and pious life—on his last
voyage when nearly seventy years of age—that Columbus, to save his
two remaining ships from foundering in the Caribbean Sea in a ter-
rible storm, had to run them ashore on the Island of Jamaica—where,
laid up for a long and miserable year—1503—he was taken very sick,
had several relapses, his men revolted, and death seem'd daily im-
minent. . . . See, the Antillean Island, with its florid skies and rich
foliage and scenery, the waves beating the solitary sands, and the
hulls of the ships in the distance. See, the figure of the great Admiral,
walking the beach . . . and hear him uttering . . ."

A batter'd, wreck'd old man,
Thrown on this savage shore, far, far from home,
Pent by the sea and dark rebellious brows, twelve dreary months,
Sore, stiff with many toils, sicken'd and nigh to death,
I take my way along the island's edge,   5
Venting a heavy heart.

I am too full of woe!
Haply I may not live another day;
I cannot rest O God, I cannot eat or drink or sleep,
Till I put forth myself, my prayer, once more to Thee,   10
Breathe, bathe myself once more in Thee, commune with Thee,
Report myself once more to Thee.

Thou knowest my years entire, my life,
My long and crowded life of active work, not adoration merely;
Thou knowest the prayers and vigils of my youth,   15
Thou knowest my manhood's solemn and visionary meditations,
Thou knowest how before I commenced I devoted all to come to
    Thee,
Thou knowest I have in age ratified all those vows and strictly
    kept them,
Thou knowest I have not once lost nor faith nor ecstasy in Thee,
In shackles, prison'd, in disgrace, repining not,   20
Accepting all from Thee, as duly come from Thee.

All my emprises have been fill'd with Thee,
My speculations, plans, begun and carried on in thought of Thee,
Sailing the deep or journeying the land for Thee;
Intentions, purports, aspirations mine, leaving results to Thee. 25

O I am sure they really came from Thee,
The urge, the ardor, the unconquerable will,
The potent, felt, interior command, stronger than words,
A message from the Heavens whispering to me even in sleep,
These sped me on.   30

By me and these the work so far accomplish'd,
By me earth's elder cloy'd and stifled lands, uncloy'd, unloos'd,
By me the hemispheres rounded and tied, the unknown to the
    known.

The end I know not, it is all in Thee,
Or small or great I know not—haply what broad fields, what
    lands,   35
Haply the brutish measureless human undergrowth I know,
Transplanted there may rise to stature, knowledge worthy Thee,
Haply the swords I know may there indeed be turn'd to reaping-
    tools,
Haply the lifeless cross I know, Europe's dead cross, may bud and
    blossom there.

One effort more, my altar this bleak sand;   40
That Thou O God my life hast lighted,

With ray of light, steady, ineffable, vouchsafed of Thee,
Light rare untellable, lighting the very light,
Beyond all signs, descriptions, languages;
For that O God, be it my latest word, here on my knees,   45
Old, poor, and paralyzed, I thank Thee.

My terminus near,
The clouds already closing in upon me,
The voyage balk'd, the course disputed, lost,
I yield my ships to Thee.   50

My hands, my limbs, grow nerveless,
My brain feels rack'd, bewildered,
Let the old timbers part, I will not part,
I will cling fast to Thee, O God, though the waves buffet me,
Thee, Thee at least I know.   55

Is it the prophet's thought I speak, or am I raving?
What do I know of life? what of myself?
I know not even my own work past or present,
Dim ever-shifting guesses of it spread before me,
Of newer better worlds, their mighty parturition,   60
Mocking, perplexing me.

And these things I see suddenly, what mean they?
As if some miracle, some hand divine unseal'd my eyes,
Shadowy vast shapes smile through the air and sky,
And on the distant waves sail countless ships,   65
And anthems in new tongues I hear saluting me.

8. *Haply:* Perhaps
19. *nor . . . nor:* neither . . . nor
22. *emprises:* enterprises, undertakings
35. *Or . . . or:* Either . . . or
42. *ineffable:* inexpressible; *vouchsafed:* given graciously

What is the value of an extemporaneous prayer of this kind in contrast with one that has been memorized and uttered?

What does this prayer reveal of the mind and character of Columbus? What dominant mood prevails?

This poem is an example of free verse that is divided into stanzas. What thought development and progression of feeling did you sense from stanza to stanza?

The diction and phrasing remind you of what other great work of literature?

PART TWO

More Lyric Verse to Read for Enjoyment

AMERICA THE BEAUTIFUL

Katharine Lee Bates

Many persons, of whom I am one, believe this beautiful poem should be America's national anthem. It is a poem to thrill every patriotic American, and inspire him to work for the achievement of the ideals which we—sometimes all too thoughtlessly—profess.

O beautiful for spacious skies,
    For amber waves of grain,
For purple mountain majesties
    Above the fruited plain!
America! America!   5
    God shed His grace on thee
And crown thy good with brotherhood
    From sea to shining sea!

O beautiful for pilgrim feet,
    Whose stern, impassioned stress   10
A thoroughfare for freedom beat
    Across the wilderness!
America! America!
    God mend thine every flaw,
Confirm thy soul in self-control,   15
    Thy liberty in law!

O beautiful for heroes proved
    In liberating strife,
Who more than self their country loved,
    And mercy more than life!   20
America! America!
    May God thy gold refine,
Till all success be nobleness
    And every gain divine!

O beautiful for patriot dream   25
    That sees beyond the years
Thine alabaster cities gleam
    Undimmed by human tears!

America! America!
God shed His grace on thee   30
And crown thy good with brotherhood
From sea to shining sea!

Name the things which make America "beautiful." Name the things
for which the poet prays.
What other patriotic poems do you know? Which is your favorite?
Why?
When you read a poem like this (or recite the "Pledge to the Flag")
do you silently vow to do your share to make America's "patriotic
dream" come true?

THE FLAG GOES BY

Henry Holcomb Bennett

Because "Old Glory" is the symbol of all the things which
made our country "America the Beautiful," respect for the flag is one
way of demonstrating true patriotism. It would be pretty hard to learn
the following poem by heart and stand unmoved when "the flag is
passing by."

Hats off!
Along the street there comes
A blare of bugles, a ruffle of drums,
A flash of color beneath the sky:
Hats off!   5
The flag is passing by!

Blue and crimson and white it shines,
Over the steel-tipped, ordered lines.
Hats off!
The colors before us fly;   10
But more than the flag is passing by.

Sea-fights and land-fights, grim and great,
Fought to make and to save the State:
Weary marches and sinking ships;
Cheers of victory on dying lips;   15

Days of plenty and years of peace;
March of a strong land's swift increase;
Equal justice, right and law,
Stately honor and reverend awe;

Sign of a nation, great and strong   20
To ward her people from foreign wrong:
Pride and glory and honor,—all
Live in the colors to stand or fall.

   Hats off!
Along the street there comes   25
A blare of bugles, a ruffle of drums;
And loyal hearts are beating high:
   Hats off!
The flag is passing by!

Which poem did you find more inspiring, Miss Bates's or Mr. Bennett's? Is your choice based on the poem's form, or content, or both?

What items could you add to Mr. Bennett's list of things for which our flag is the symbol?

By all means commit at least one of these poems to memory.

IN FLANDERS FIELDS

Lieutenant-Colonel John McCrae

Perhaps the best-known poem to come out of World War One is the following rondeau. It reminds us that it is our duty to see that our dead who sleep in Flanders fields shall not have died in vain.

In Flanders fields the poppies blow
Between the crosses, row on row,
   That mark our place; and in the sky
   The larks, still bravely singing, fly
Scarce heard amid the guns below.   5

We are the Dead. Short days ago
We lived, felt dawn, saw sunset glow,
   Loved and were loved, and now we lie
   In Flanders fields.

Take up our quarrel with the foe;   10
To you from failing hands we throw
    The torch; be yours to hold it high.
    If ye break faith with us who die
We shall not sleep, though poppies grow
    In Flanders fields.   15

Exactly what is "our quarrel with the foe"? What is the "torch" the symbol of?

The *rondeau* is one of the simpler French forms: a poem of three stanzas with two rimes and a refrain: *aabba aabc aabbac*. The two *c*'s (verses 9 and 15) are the refrain, which is a repetition of the first half of the first verse.

If you wish to try your hand at writing a rondeau, study the form as illustrated by "In Flanders Fields."

I HAVE A RENDEZVOUS WITH DEATH

Alan Seeger

This famous poem, written during World War One, gained added significance by the death of the poet in action.

I have a rendezvous with Death
    At some disputed barricade
    When Spring comes round with rustling shade
And apple blossoms fill the air.
    I have a rendezvous with Death   5
When Spring brings back blue days and fair.

It may be he shall take my hand
And lead me into his dark land
    And close my eyes and quench my breath;
It may be I shall pass him still.   10
    I have a rendezvous with Death
On some scarred slope of battered hill,
    When Spring comes round again this year
    And the first meadow flowers appear.

God knows 'twere better to be deep   15
    Pillowed in silk and scented down,

Where love throbs out in blissful sleep,
   Pulse nigh to pulse, and breath to breath,
   Where hushed awakenings are dear . . .
But I've a rendezvous with Death   20
   At midnight in some flaming town,
When Spring trips north again this year,
   And I to my pledged word am true,
   I shall not fail that rendezvous.

Why was the rendezvous with death to be in the spring? What part of speech is *down* in line 16? Why are Death and Spring capitalized? What emotion do you think Alan Seeger is expressing in this poem? What have you learned from this poem that might help you to face death philosophically?

THE SOLDIER

Rupert Brooke

        This sonnet is still another poem written during World War One. It, too, gained fame because its author, a Royal Navy officer, died while on duty before the war had ended. It is a touching expression of a youthful Englishman's love of country: his body shall enrich "some corner of a foreign field" because it is an English body; his soul shall enrich "the eternal mind" because it is an English soul.

If I should die, think only this of me:
   That there's some corner of a foreign field
That is for ever England. There shall be
   In that rich earth a richer dust concealed;
A dust whom England bore, shaped, made aware,   5
   Gave, once, her flowers to love, her ways to roam,
A body of England's, breathing English air,
   Washed by the rivers, blest by suns of home.

And think, this heart, all evil shed away,
   A pulse in the eternal mind, no less   10
   Gives somewhere back the thoughts by England given;
Her sights and sounds; dreams happy as her day;
   And laughter, learnt of friends; and gentleness,
   In hearts at peace, under an English heaven.

What emotional effect did this poem have on you? Tell why you
do, or do not, feel toward America as Rupert Brooke felt toward Eng-
land.

What would you list as *American* gifts to your body and your heart?

CONCORD HYMN

Ralph Waldo Emerson

At Concord, Massachusetts, on April 19, 1775, patriotic cit-
izens, guns in hand, stood their ground in the defense of liberty from
the encroachment of tyranny. On April 19, 1836, a monument was
dedicated to these brave "minute men" of the American Revolution.
For this occasion, the first citizen of Concord, Ralph Waldo Emer-
son, wrote the following poem, which immortalized the "embattled
farmers" as those who "fired the shot heard round the world."

By the rude bridge that arched the flood,
　　Their flag to April's breeze unfurled,
Here once the embattled farmers stood,
　　And fired the shot heard round the world.

The foe long since in silence slept;　　　　　　　　　　　5
　　Alike the conqueror silent sleeps;
And Time the ruined bridge has swept
　　Down the dark stream which seaward creeps.

On this green bank, by this soft stream,
　　We set to-day a votive stone;　　　　　　　　　　　10
That memory may their deed redeem,
　　When, like our sires, our sons are gone.

Spirit, that made those heroes dare
　　To die, and leave their children free,
Bid Time and Nature gently spare　　　　　　　　　　15
　　The shaft we raise to them and thee.

What is a "votive stone"? What does Emerson say was the reason
for setting up the Concord monument? To whom is the last stanza
addressed?

How effective do you think monuments are in accomplishing their
purpose: "that memory may their deed redeem"? Which has probably
done more to keep alive the memory of "embattled farmers"—the
monument or this poem?

ODE *

Sung on the Occasion of Decorating the Graves of the
Confederate Dead, at Magnolia Cemetery, Charleston, S. C.

Henry Timrod

In this well-known "Ode" Timrod points out that tears and
flowers are really greater tributes to heroic dead than marble columns.

Sleep sweetly in your humble graves,—
  Sleep, martyrs of a fallen cause!
Though yet no marble column craves
  The pilgrim here to pause,

In seeds of laurel in the earth   5
  The blossom of your fame is blown,
And somewhere, waiting for its birth,
  The shaft is in the stone!

Meanwhile, behalf the tardy years
  Which keep in trust your storied tombs,   10
Behold! your sisters bring their tears,
  And these memorial blooms.

Small tributes! but your shades will smile
  More proudly on these wreaths to-day,
Than when some cannon-moulded pile   15
  Shall overlook this bay.

Stoop, angels, hither from the skies!
  There is no holier spot of ground
Than where defeated valor lies,
  By mourning beauty crowned!   20

Be sure you understand what the poet means by saying the blossom
blooms ("is blown") in the seed, and "the shaft is in the stone;" also
by "storied tombs," "some cannon-moulded pile."

Why do you agree, or disagree, with the statement made in the last
three lines?

* An *ode* is a serious poem of rich and elevated thought, written in various
forms.

FOUR THINGS

Henry Van Dyke

Here is a little five-line poem well worth memorizing.

> Four things a man must learn to do
> If he would make his record true:
> To think without confusion clearly;
> To love his fellow-men sincerely;
> To act from honest motives purely;   5
> To trust in God and Heaven securely.

Reduce the "four things" to one word each. What four things would you list for a man to do to "make his record true"?

BE STRONG

Maltbie Davenport Babcock

If we are to do our share in righting the world's wrongs we must have strength. The victory is not to the weak.

> Be strong!
> We are not here to play, to dream, to drift;
> We have hard work to do, and loads to lift;
> Shun not the struggle—face it; 'tis God's gift.

> Be strong!   5
> Say not, "The days are evil. Who's to blame?"
> And fold the hands and acquiesce—oh shame!
> Stand up, speak out, and bravely, in God's name.

> Be strong!
> It matters not how deep intrenched the wrong,   10
> How hard the battle goes, the day how long;
> Faint not—fight on! To-morrow comes the song.

What does the poet mean by "God's gift," "fold the hands and acquiesce," "the song"?

INVICTUS

William Ernest Henley

This proud assertion that man's soul is unconquerable is one of
the best-known poems in the English language.

> Out of the night that covers me,
>   Black as the Pit from pole to pole,
> I thank whatever gods may be
>   For my unconquerable soul.
>
> In the fell clutch of circumstance   5
>   I have not winced nor cried aloud.
> Under the bludgeonings of chance
>   My head is bloody, but unbowed.
>
> Beyond this place of wrath and tears
>   Looms but the horror of the shade,   10
> And yet the menace of the years
>   Finds, and shall find me, unafraid.
>
> It matters not how strait the gate,
>   How charged with punishments the scroll,
> I am the master of my fate;   15
>   I am the captain of my soul.

5. *fell:* cruel
13. *strait:* narrow

What about the poet's life can you infer from this poem?
Shakespeare put it this way:

> The fault, dear Brutus, is not in our stars,
> But in ourselves, that we are underlings.

Which wording do you prefer?

THANKSGIVING EVE

Grantland Rice

If, on Thanksgiving Eve, we should stop to count our bless-
ings, each would make a different list. Here is a little list you might

well store in your memory to serve you later in life, if ever fate should
be rough to you and despair seem stronger than faith and hope.

> Thanks for the little and the simpler things
>   That only average fellows ever know,
> The few breaks, now and then, that rough fate brings
>   To scatter sunlight over winter's snow.
> The grip of hand—a quick smile, here and there,   5
>   A friend or two along roads rough and crude,
> And more than all in facing life's despair
>   Thanks for the golden gift of fortitude.

What could you add to the poet's short list of the "simpler things"
known only to "average fellows"?

What are the comparisons in lines 3 and 4—in "breaks," "sunlight,"
"winter's snow"?

What exactly is fortitude? Would it be first on your list of "golden
gifts"? If not, what would have priority?

GOD OF OUR FATHERS
Daniel Crane Roberts

Some of the most beautiful lyrics are those which have been
set to music and are sung in our churches. "God of Our Fathers" is a
hymn which expresses feelings common to persons of most religious
faiths.

> God of our fathers, whose almighty hand
> Leads forth in beauty all the starry band
> Of shining worlds in splendor through the skies,
> Our grateful songs before thy throne arise.
>
> Thy love divine hath led us in the past,   5
> In this free land by thee our lot is cast;
> Be thou our ruler, guardian, guide, and stay,
> Thy word our law, thy paths our chosen way.
>
> From war's alarms, from deadly pestilence,
> Be thy strong arm our ever sure defence;   10
> The true religion in our hearts increase,
> Thy bounteous goodness nourish us in peace.

120

Refresh thy people on their toilsome way,
Lead us from night to never-ending day;
Fill all our lives with love and grace divine,   15
And glory, laud, and praise be ever thine.

Which lines did you find most impressive? Which ones would you like to change?

Name some hymns which are among your favorites. When you sing a hymn, what is lost if you do not give thought to the words?

Two Psalms

No greater religious songs exist than the Psalms of the Bible. The most famous one is, of course, Psalm 23: The Lord Is My Shepherd. Here are two others familiar to most persons.

PSALM 100

Make a joyful noise unto the Lord, all ye lands.
Serve the Lord with gladness: come before his presence with singing.
Know ye that the Lord he is God: it is he that hath made us, and not we ourselves; we are his people, and the sheep of his pasture.
Enter into his gates with thanksgiving, and into his courts with praise: be thankful unto him, and bless his name.
For the Lord is good; his mercy is everlasting; and his truth endureth to all generations.   5

PSALM 121

I will lift up mine eyes unto the hills, from whence cometh my help.
My help cometh from the Lord, which made heaven and earth.
He will not suffer thy foot to be moved: he that keepeth thee will not slumber.

Behold, he that keepeth Israel shall neither slumber nor sleep.

The Lord is thy keeper; the Lord is thy shade upon thy right hand. 5

The sun shall not smite thee by day, nor the moon by night.

The Lord shall preserve thee from all evil: he shall preserve thy soul.

The Lord shall preserve thy going out and thy coming in from this time forth, and even for evermore.

THE INVESTMENT

Robert Frost

In this poem, Robert Frost, in a characteristic sly and quiet way, is admonishing you about marriage which, he thinks, should mean more than being merely Mr. and Mrs. Let the poem penetrate; "it may serve a turn in your life."

Over back where they speak of life as staying
("You couldn't call it living, for it ain't"),
There was an old, old house renewed with paint,
And in it a piano loudly playing.

Out in the ploughed ground in the cold a digger, 5
Among unearthed potatoes standing still,
Was counting winter dinners, one a hill,
With half an ear to the piano's vigor.

All that piano and new paint back there,
Was it some money suddenly come into? 10
Or some extravagance young love had been to?
Or old love on an impulse not to care—

Not to sink under being man and wife,
But get some color and music out of life?

What are the thoughts that pass through the mind of the potato digger? What is the meaning of the interplay between the old and the new? What meaning do the words *color* and *music* take on?

In form (meter and rime scheme) what really is the poem?

HOME, SWEET HOME

John Howard Payne

Some sweetly sentimental poems live on, decade after decade, in spite of scorn of pessimists and cynics. Such a poem is "Home, Sweet Home," which was the theme song of a popular drama over a hundred years ago and still has power to pull at our heart-strings.

Mid pleasures and palaces though we may roam,
Be it ever so humble, there's no place like home;
A charm from the sky seems to hallow us there,
Which, seek through the world, is ne'er met with elsewhere.
Home, home, sweet, sweet home!   5
There's no place like home, oh, there's no place like home!

An exile from home, splendor dazzles in vain;
Oh, give me my lowly thatched cottage again!
The birds singing gayly, that came at my call—
Give me them—and the peace of mind, dearer than all!   10
Home, home, sweet, sweet home!
There's no place like home, oh, there's no place like home!

I gaze on the moon as I tread the drear wild,
And feel that my mother now thinks of her child,
As she looks on that moon from our own cottage door   15
Thro' the woodbine, whose fragrance shall cheer me no more.
Home, home, sweet, sweet home!
There's no place like home, oh, there's no place like home!

How sweet 'tis to sit 'neath a fond father's smile,
And the caress of a mother to soothe and beguile!   20
Let others delight mid new pleasures to roam,
But give me, oh, give me, the pleasures of home,
Home, home, sweet, sweet home!
There's no place like home, oh, there's no place like home!

To thee I'll return, overburdened with care;   25
The heart's dearest solace will smile on me there;
No more from that cottage again will I roam;

Be it ever so humble, there's no place like home.
Home, home, sweet, sweet home!
There's no place like home, oh, there's no place like home!   30

What is the difference between *sentiment* and *sentimentality?*
Which do you think this poem exemplifies?
What characteristics of this "sweet home" are lacking in many
modern homes? What has caused this change? What effect does it
have upon character and conduct?

THE OLD OAKEN BUCKET
Samuel Woodworth

Like "Home, Sweet Home," "The Old Oaken Bucket" was
written over a hundred years ago and has a secure place in the Ameri-
can cultural heritage.

How dear to my heart are the scenes of my childhood,
    When fond recollection presents them to view!
The orchard, the meadow, the deep-tangled wildwood,
    And every loved spot which my infancy knew,
The wide-spreading pond and the mill which stood by it,   5
    The bridge and the rock where the cataract fell;
The cot of my father, the dairy house nigh it,
    And e'en the rude-bucket which hung in the well.
The old oaken bucket, the iron-bound bucket,
The moss-covered bucket which hung in the well.   10

That moss-covered vessel I hail as a treasure;
    For often at noon, when returned from the field,
I found it the source of an exquisite pleasure,
    The purest and sweetest that nature can yield.
How ardent I seized it with hands that were glowing!   15
    And quick to the white-pebbled bottom it fell;
Then soon, with the emblem of truth overflowing,
    And dripping with coolness it rose from the well;
The old oaken bucket, the iron-bound bucket,
The moss-covered bucket, arose from the well.   20

How sweet from the green mossy brim to receive it,
　As poised on the curb, it inclined to my lips!
Not a full blushing goblet could tempt me to leave it,
　Though filled with the nectar that Jupiter sips.
And now, far removed from the loved situation,　　　25
　The tear of regret will intrusively swell,
As fancy reverts to my father's plantation,
　And sighs for the bucket which hangs in the well;
The old oaken bucket, the iron-bound bucket,
The moss-covered bucket which hangs in the well.　　30

　Apply your test for sentiment *versus* sentimentality to this poem.
Quote from the poem to defend your conclusions.
　What particular object in the environment of your childhood or
youth is "dear to your heart"? Try to put this "fond recollection" into
words.

WOODMAN, SPARE THAT TREE

George P. Morris

　　This poem, another "old timer," records not only stored-up
memories of a happy childhood, but the natural resentment to the
destruction of those things around which our heart-strings cling.

　　Woodman, spare that tree!
　　Touch not a single bough!
　　In youth it sheltered me,
　　And I'll protect it now.
　　'Twas my forefather's hand　　　5
　　That placed it near his cot;
　　There, woodman, let it stand
　　Thy ax shall harm it not!

　　That old familiar tree,
　　Whose glory and renown　　　10
　　Are spread o'er land and sea,
　　And wouldst thou hew it down?
　　Woodman, forbear thy stroke!
　　Cut not its earth-bound ties!

125

Oh! spare that aged oak,   15
Now towering to the skies.

When but an idle boy
I sought its grateful shade;
In all their gushing joy
Here too my sisters played.   20
My mother kissed me here
My father pressed my hand—
Forgive this foolish tear,
But let that old oak stand!

My heart-strings round thee cling,   25
Close as thy bark, old friend!
Here shall the wild-bird sing,
And still thy branches bend.
Old tree, the storm still brave!
And, woodman, leave the spot!   30
While I've a hand to save,
Thy ax shall harm it not.

In what way is this poem a clear example of heart rather than mind?
What is your attitude toward the author's intense emotion? Is it senti-
ment or sentimentality? Which would you rather be, overly sentimen-
tal or overly cold-blooded?

For another poet's reaction to the cutting down of trees see "The
Trees Are Down," page 161.

THE HOUSE BY THE SIDE OF THE ROAD

Sam Walter Foss

This poem quickly caught the popular fancy and is often and
widely quoted. The friendliness, humility, and tolerance expressed in
it win approving response from most persons, whose hearts also are
filled with good will to men.

There are hermit souls that live withdrawn
In the place of their self-content;
There are souls like stars, that dwell apart,
In a fellowless firmament;

There are pioneer souls that blaze their paths 5
Where highways never ran—
But let me live by the side of the road
And be a friend to man.

Let me live in a house by the side of the road,
Where the race of men go by— 10
The men who are good and the men who are bad,
As good and as bad as I.
I would not sit in the scorner's seat,
Or hurl the cynic's ban—
Let me live in a house by the side of the road 15
And be a friend to man.

I see from my house by the side of the road,
By the side of the highway of life,
The men who press with the ardor of hope,
The men who are faint with the strife. 20
But I turn not away from their smiles nor their tears,
Both parts of an infinite plan—
Let me live in a house by the side of the road
And be a friend to man.

I know there are brook-gladdened meadows ahead, 25
And mountains of wearisome height;
That the road passes on through the long afternoon
And stretches away to the night.
But still I rejoice when the travelers rejoice,
And weep with the strangers that moan, 30
Nor live in my house by the side of the road
Like a man who dwells alone.

Let me live in my house by the side of the road,
It's here the race of men go by—
They are good, they are bad, they are weak, they are strong, 35
Wise, foolish—so am I;
Then why should I sit in the scorner's seat,
Or hurl the cynic's ban?
Let me live in my house by the side of the road
And be a friend to man. 40

Point out lines in the poem which indicate that the author is not just a spectator of the lives of others, that he is not a "hermit soul" but really "a friend to man."

How about yourself? Do you sit in the scorner's seat? If so, which of the persons mentioned do you feel you have a right to scorn?

Would you say that the author lacks ambition? If so, do you consider this lack a serious fault? Defend your answer.

THE ARROW AND THE SONG

Henry Wadsworth Longfellow

There are few poems of which we say, "This is a poem every one knows." This common knowledge of poems (and short stories, and novels, and plays, and legends) binds us together with what we call our "literary heritage." "The Arrow and the Song" is such a poem.

I shot an arrow into the air,
It fell to earth, I knew not where;
For, so swiftly it flew, the sight
Could not follow it in its flight.

I breathed a song into the air, 5
It fell to earth, I knew not where;
For who has sight so keen and strong,
That it can follow the flight of song?

Long, long afterward, in an oak
I found the arrow, still unbroke; 10
And the song, from beginning to end,
I found again in the heart of a friend.

What is the message of the poem? What lesson can we learn from it?

This is a poem you will surely wish to commit to memory.

THE VILLAGE BLACKSMITH

Henry Wadsworth Longfellow

Though the village smithy is now so difficult to find that it has become just a romantic spot sought out by tourists, Longfellow's poem has a secure place in America's literary heritage.

Even if you have read the poem before, read it again and discover whether your added knowledge of lyric poetry enables you to get more pleasure from the poem than you did as a child.

Under a spreading chestnut-tree
  The village smithy stands;
The smith, a mighty man is he,
  With large and sinewy hands;
And the muscles of his brawny arms   5
  Are strong as iron bands.

His hair is crisp, and black, and long,
  His face is like the tan;
His brow is wet with honest sweat,
  He earns whate'er he can,   10
And looks the whole world in the face,
  For he owes not any man.

Week in, week out, from morn till night,
  You can hear his bellows blow;
You can hear him swing his heavy sledge   15
  With measured beat and slow,
Like a sexton ringing the village bell,
  When the evening sun is low.

And children coming home from school
  Look in at the open door;   20
They love to see the flaming forge,
  And hear the bellows roar,
And catch the burning sparks that fly
  Like chaff from a threshing-floor.

He goes on Sunday to the church,   25
  And sits among his boys;
He hears the parson pray and preach,
  He hears his daughter's voice,
Singing in the village choir,
  And it makes his heart rejoice.   30

It sounds to him like her mother's voice,
  Singing in Paradise!
He needs must think of her once more,

How in the grave she lies;
And with his hard, rough hand he wipes   35
A tear out of his eyes.

Toiling,—rejoicing,—sorrowing,
  Onward through life he goes;
Each morning sees some task begun,
  Each evening sees its close;   40
Something attempted, something done,
  Has earned a night's repose.

Thanks, thanks to thee, my worthy friend,
  For the lesson thou hast taught!
Thus at the flaming forge of life   45
  Our fortunes must be wrought;
Thus on its sounding anvil shaped
  Each burning deed and thought!

List the blacksmith's virtues as presented by Longfellow. State in
your own words the lesson that he taught.

THE SONG OF THE THRUSH

T. A. Daly

In this poem nature is bursting with the song of spring, and an
Irish immigrant enjoys this, too. But not wholly so, for when he
hears the song of the thrush there comes to him a natural nostalgia
for the days of yore in his homeland. The poet very touchingly brings
out this contrast in a person who is glad to be here in the U.S.A. but
who also has happy memories of his native country, especially its
natural beauty.

Ah! the May was grand this mornin'!
  Shure, how could I feel forlorn in
Such a land, when tree and flower tossed their kisses to the breeze?
  Could an Irish heart be quiet
  While the Spring was runnin' riot,   5
An' the birds of free America were singin' in the trees?
  In the songs that they were singin'
  No familiar note was ringin',

But I strove to imitate them an' I whistled like a lad.
> Oh, my heart was warm to love them 10
> For the very newness of them—
For the ould songs that they helped me to forget—an' I was glad.

> So I mocked the feathered choir
> To my hungry heart's desire,
An' I gloried in the comradeship that made their joy my own. 15
> Till a new note sounded, stillin'
> All the rest. A thrush was trillin'!
Ah, the thrush I left behind me in the fields about Athlone!
> Where, upon the whitethorn swayin',
> He was minstrel of the Mayin', 20
In my days of love an' laughter that the years have laid at rest;
> Here again his notes were ringin'!
> But I'd lost the heart for singin'—
Ah, the song I could not answer was the one I knew the best.

What is the meaning of the last line? Why could not the man answer the song he knew the best?

How does the poem characterize the person saying it?

What other poems concerned with homesickness do you know?

THE HOUSE ON THE HILL

Edwin Arlington Robinson

To express his feelings about the abandoned house on the hill, Edwin Arlington Robinson chose the familiar French verse form known as the *villanelle*. The villanelle is artificial and fairly complex, but it gives a disarming impression of simplicity and spontaneity.

> They are all gone away,
> The House is shut and still,
> There is nothing more to say.

> Through broken walls and gray
> The winds blow bleak and shrill: 5
> They are all gone away.

Nor is there one to-day
    To speak them good or ill:
There is nothing more to say.

Why is it then we stray   10
    Around that sunken sill?
They are all gone away.

And our poor fancy-play
    For them is wasted skill:
There is nothing more to say.   15

There is ruin and decay
    In the House on the Hill:
They are all gone away,
There is nothing more to say.

As far as you were concerned, in what way did the artificial French
form help or hinder the poet in communicating his emotion?

Write out a clear definition of a villanelle (nineteen lines, five ter-
cets, one quatrain, two rimes, a certain rime scheme, certain repeti-
tions).

What is a *refrain?* Which lines in a villanelle are refrain?

Try your hand at writing a villanelle. (Or a rondeau. See page
114.)

MEMORY

Abraham Lincoln

In a letter (April 18, 1846) to his friend Andrew Johnston,
a lawyer of Quincy, Illinois, Lincoln wrote: "In the fall of 1844, think-
ing I might aid some to carry the state of Indiana for Mr. Clay, I
went into the neighborhood in that state in which I was raised, where
my mother and only sister were buried, and from which I had been
absent about fifteen years. That part of the country is, within itself,
as unpoetical as any spot of the earth; but still, seeing it and its objects
and inhabitants aroused feelings in me which were certainly poetry;
though whether my expression of those feelings is poetry is quite an-
other question. When I got to writing, the change of subjects divided
the thing into four little divisions or cantos, the first only of which I
send you now . . ."

My childhood's home I see again,
And sadden with the view;
And still, as memory crowds my brain,
There's pleasure in it, too.

O memory! thou midway world 5
'Twixt earth and paradise,
Where things decayed and loved ones lost
In dreamy shadows rise,

And, freed from all that's earthly, vile,
Seem hallowed, pure and bright, 10
Like scenes in some enchanted isle
All bathed in liquid light.

As dusky mountains please the eye
When twilight chases day;
As bugle notes that, passing by, 15
In distance die away;

As, leaving some grand waterfall,
We, lingering, list its roar—
So memory will hallow all
We've known but know no more. 20

Near twenty years have passed away
Since here I bid farewell
To woods and fields, and scenes of play,
And playmates loved so well.

Where many were, but few remain 25
Of old familiar things,
But seeing them to mind again
The lost and absent brings.

The friends I left that parting day,
How changed, as time has sped! 30
Young childhood grown, strong manhood gray;
And half of all are dead.

I hear the loved survivors tell
   How nought from death could save,
Till every sound appears a knell   35
   And every spot a grave.

I range the fields with pensive tread,
   And pace the hollow rooms,
And feel (companion of the dead)
   I'm living in the tombs.   40

What did Lincoln mean by "an unpoetical spot"? Why were the feelings it aroused poetry to him? Do you think his "expression of those feelings" is good, or poor, verse? Why?

Note the three things to which memory is compared in stanzas 4 and 5. Which one do you like best?

SWEET AND LOW

Alfred Tennyson

No lyrics are more musical than the lullabies; and no lullaby is more lovely than Tennyson's "Sweet and Low."

Sweet and low, sweet and low,
   Wind of the western sea,
Low, low, breathe and blow,
   Wind of the western sea!
   Over the rolling waters go,   5
   Come from the dying moon, and blow,
   Blow him again to me;
While my little one, while my pretty one sleeps.

Sleep and rest, sleep and rest,
   Father will come to thee soon;   10
Rest, rest, on mother's breast,
Father will come to thee soon;
   Father will come to his babe in the nest,
   Silver sails all out of the west
   Under the silver moon;   15
Sleep, my little one, sleep, my pretty one, sleep.

What do the absence and the probable occupation of the father
add to the emotional impact of this poem?

SWEETES' LI'L' FELLER

Frank L. Stanton

This lullaby concentrates on the beauty of the babe rather
than the absence of the father, as in "Sweet and Low."

Sweetes' li'l' feller—
Everybody knows;
Dunno what ter call 'im,
But he mighty lak' a rose!

Lookin' at his mammy   5
Wid eyes so shiny-blue,
Mek' you think dat heaven
Is comin' clost ter you!

W'en he's dar a-sleepin'
In his li'l' place,   10
Think I see de angels
Lookin' thoo' de lace.

W'en de dark is fallin'—
W'en de shadders creep,
Den dey comes on tip-toe   15
Ter kiss 'im in his sleep.

Sweetes' li'l' feller—
Everybody knows;
Dunno what ter call 'im,
But he mighty lak' a rose!   20

What does the dialect add to the poem?
If you were asked to paint pictures to illustrate this poem and
"Sweet and Low," how would the two pictures differ?

Five Poems from A Child's Garden of Verses

Robert Louis Stevenson

Is *A Child's Garden of Verses* a part of your childhood memories? If so, you will enjoy reading again some of the lyrics you knew as a child; if not, these poems will introduce you to the most famous book of children's verse in the world—except, of course, *Mother Goose.*

BED IN SUMMER

In winter I get up at night
And dress by yellow candle-light.
In summer, quite the other way,
I have to go to bed by day.

I have to go to bed and see   5
The birds still hopping on the tree,
Or hear the grown-up people's feet
Still going past me in the street.

And does it not seem hard to you,
When all the sky is clear and blue,   10
And I should like so much to play,
To have to go to bed by day?

WINDY NIGHTS

Whenever the moon and stars are set,
    Whenever the wind is high,
All night long in the dark and wet,
    A man goes riding by.
Late in the night when the fires are out,   5
Why does he gallop and gallop about?

Whenever the trees are crying aloud,
    And ships are tossed at sea,
By, on the highway, low and loud,
    By at the gallop goes he.   10
By at the gallop he goes, and then
By he comes back at the gallop again.

SYSTEM

Every night my prayers I say,
And get my dinner every day;
And every day that I've been good,
I get an orange after food.

The child that is not clean and neat,   5
With lots of toys and things to eat,
He is a naughty child, I'm sure—
Or else his dear papa is poor.

THE SWING

How do you like to go up in a swing,
    Up in the air so blue?
Oh, I do think it the pleasantest thing
    Ever a child can do!

Up in the air and over the wall,   5
    Till I can see so wide,
Rivers and trees and cattle and all
    Over the countryside—

Till I look down on the garden green,
    Down on the roof so brown—   10
Up in the air I go flying again,
    Up in the air and down!

LOOKING-GLASS RIVER

Smooth it slides upon its travel
Here a wimple, there a gleam—
O the clean gravel!
O the smooth stream!

Sailing blossoms, silver fishes,   5
Paven pools as clear as air—
How a child wishes
To live down there!

We can see our colored faces
Floating on the shaken pool   10
Down in cool places,
Dim and very cool;

Till a wind or water wrinkle,
Dipping marten, plumping trout,
Spreads in a twinkle   15
And blots all out.

See the rings pursue each other;
All below grows black as night
Just as if mother
Had blown out the light!   20

Patience, children, just a minute—
See the spreading circles die;
The stream and all in it
Will clear by-and-by.

Point out in these selections examples of humor, emotional outlet, skillful musical effects, delightful imagery, and good advice.

THE MODERN HIAWATHA

George A. Strong

When he killed the Mudjokivis,
Of the skin he made him mittens,

Made them with the fur side inside
Made them with the skin side outside,
He, to get the warm side inside, 5
Put the inside skin side outside;
He, to get the cold side outside,
Put the warm side fur side inside.
That's why he put the fur side inside,
Why he put the skin side outside 10
Why he turned them inside outside.

SEEIN' THINGS

Eugene Field

Eugene Field was a popular American poet of the late nineteenth century. Probably you are familiar with his most famous poem, "Little Boy Blue," and perhaps some of his lullabies like "A Dutch Lullaby" ("Wynken, Blynken, and Nod"). One of his most famous humorous poems is "Seein' Things," which must be read aloud to bring out the wit and gentle satire.

I ain't afeard uv snakes, or toads, or bugs, or worms, or mice,
An' things 'at girls are skeered uv I think are awful nice!
I'm pretty brave, I guess; an' yet I hate to go to bed,
For, when I'm tucked up warm an' snug an' when my prayers are
     said,
Mother tells me, "Happy Dreams!" an' takes away the light, 5
An' leaves me lyin' all alone an' seein' things at night!

Sometimes they're in the corner, sometimes they're by the door,
Sometimes they're all a-standin' in the middle uv the floor;
Sometimes they are a-sittin' down, sometimes they're walkin'
     round
So softly and so creepylike they never make a sound! 10
Sometimes they are as black as ink, an' other times they're
     white—
But the color ain't no difference when you see things at night!

Once when I licked a feller 'at had just moved on our street,
An' father sent me up to bed without a bite to eat,
I woke up in the dark an' saw things standin' in a row, 15

139

A-lookin' at me cross-eyed an' p'intin' at me—so!
Oh, my! I wuz so skeered that time I never slep' a mite—
It's almost alluz when I'm bad I see things at night!

Lucky thing I ain't a girl, or I'd be skeered to death!
Bein' I'm a boy, I duck my head an' hold my breath;   20
An' I am, oh, *so* sorry I'm a naughty boy, an' then
I promise to be better an' I say my prayers again!
Gran'ma tells me that's the only way to make it right
When a feller has been wicked an' sees things at night!

An' so when other naughty boys would coax me into sin,   25
I try to skwush the Tempter's voice 'at urges me within;
An' when they's pie for supper, or cakes 'at's big and nice,
I want to—but I do not pass my plate f'r them things twice!
No, ruther let Starvation wipe me slowly out of sight
Than I should keep a-livin' on an' seein' things at night!   30

Show how the poem, though written about a little boy, has appeal
for older persons. A famous contemporary of Field was James Whit-
comb Riley. Find volumes of Field's and Riley's poems and read to the
class some which you found amusing.

THE TWELVE DAYS OF CHRISTMAS
Anonymous

If you are not familiar with this famous old Christmas cumu-
lative jingle, now is the time to learn it.

The first day of Christmas,
My true love sent to me
A partridge in a pear tree.

The second day of Christmas,
My true love sent to me   5
Two turtle doves, and
A partridge in a pear tree.

The third day of Christmas,
My true love sent to me
Three French hens,   10

Two turtle doves, and
A partridge in a pear tree.

The fourth day of Christmas,
My true love sent to me
Four colly birds,   15
Three French hens,
Two turtle doves, and
A partridge in a pear tree.

The fifth day of Christmas,
My true love sent to me   20
Five gold rings,
Four colly birds,
Three French hens,
Two turtle doves, and
A partridge in a pear tree.   25

The sixth day of Christmas,
My true love sent to me
Six geese a-laying,
Five gold rings,
Four colly birds,   30
Three French hens,
Two turtle doves, and
A partridge in a pear tree.

The seventh day of Christmas,
My true love sent to me   35
Seven swans a-swimming,
Six geese a-laying,
Five gold rings,
Four colly birds,
Three French hens,   40
Two turtle doves, and
A partridge in a pear tree.

The eighth day of Christmas,
My true love sent to me
Eight maids a-milking,   45

Seven swans a-swimming,
Six geese a-laying,
Five gold rings,
Four colly birds,
Three French hens,   50
Two turtle doves, and
A partridge in a pear tree.

The ninth day of Christmas,
My true love sent to me
Nine drummers drumming,   55
Eight maids a-milking,
Seven swans a-swimming,
Six geese a-laying,
Five gold rings,
Four colly birds,   60
Three French hens,
Two turtle doves, and
A partridge in a pear tree.

The tenth day of Christmas,
My true love sent to me   65
Ten pipers piping,
Nine drummers drumming,
Eight maids a-milking,
Seven swans a-swimming,
Six geese a-laying,   70
Five gold rings,
Four colly birds,
Three French hens,
Two turtle doves, and
A partridge in a pear tree.   75

The eleventh day of Christmas,
My true love sent to me
Eleven ladies dancing,
Ten pipers piping,
Nine drummers drumming,   80
Eight maids a-milking,

Seven swans a-swimming,
Six geese a-laying,
Five gold rings,
Four colly birds,   85
Three French hens,
Two turtle doves, and
A partridge in a pear tree.

The twelfth day of Christmas,
My true love sent to me   90
Twelve lords a-leaping,
Eleven ladies dancing,
Ten pipers piping,
Nine drummers drumming,
Eight maids a-milking,   95
Seven swans a-swimming,
Six geese a-laying,
Five gold rings,
Four colly birds,
Three French hens,   100
Two turtle doves, and
A partridge in a pear tree.

Why are all the presents appropriate gifts from a "truc love"?

THE MONTHS
Christina Rossetti

This poem carries the reader through a year in charming
couplets.

January cold desolate;
February dripping wet;
March wind rages;
April changes;
Birds sing in tune   5
To flowers of May,
And sunny June
Brings longest day;

143

In scorched July
The storm-clouds fly,   10
Lightning-torn;
August bears corn,
September fruit;
In rough October
Earth must disrobe her;   15
Stars fall and shoot
In keen November;
And night is long
And cold is strong
In bleak December.   20

Which of the months do you think Christina Rossetti has presented
well? Which ones poorly?

If you think poems like this are easy to write, try your hand at a
short poem giving the basic significance of each month. The difficulty
may surprise you.

TRAVEL

Edna St. Vincent Millay

When you hear an airplane, do you wish you were on it?
When you see a bus, a boat, a train, do you get "itchy feet"?

The railroad track is miles away,
And the day is loud with voices speaking;
Yet there isn't a train goes by all day
But I hear its whistle shrieking.

All night there isn't a train goes by,   5
Though the night is still for sleep and dreaming,
But I see its cinders red on the sky,
And hear its engine steaming.

My heart is warm with the friends I make,
And better friends I'll not be knowing,   10
Yet there isn't a train I wouldn't take,
No matter where it's going.

144

What is the meaning of *but* in lines four and seven?

In the last stanza, do you think the poet is thinking beyond a literal train to the paths leading to adventure and experience? If so, does this add to your enjoyment of the poem, or lessen it? What will determine your answer?

OLD CLOSET

Selma Robinson

On page 28 you read a poem expressing wonder at the passing of an infatuation. Here is a lighter bit of verse on the same theme.

Long ago, I tucked away
Things I thought I'd need some day:
Tarnished shoes with heels of gold;
Faded perfume, like an old
Ineffectual caress   5
In a limp, forgotten dress;
And in a box behind a bonnet
I saved a sad, uneven sonnet
That made a simple music of
Such words as love and dove and glove,   10
And a note without a name;
It read: "Nobody is to blame
That loves will end and hearts will break."
It read: "Be happy for my sake.
We've had our penny, and we've spent it."   15

I wish I could recall who sent it!

How do you think the writer feels about finding these things she has saved? How meaningful do you believe notes written today in high-school yearbooks will be ten years from now? Twenty years from now?

Find a simile and a metaphor. What are compared in each? What is your opinion of each figure?

Find an example of feminine rime.

THE DAY IS DONE

Henry Wadsworth Longfellow

In this selection, America's most loved poet expresses beautifully the peace of mind and release from worry and tension which can come from reading the "wonderful melodies" of the "humbler poets."

The day is done, and the darkness
    Falls from the wings of Night,
As a feather is wafted downward
    From an eagle in his flight.

I see the lights of the village   5
    Gleam through the rain and the mist,
And a feeling of sadness comes o'er me
    That my soul cannot resist:

A feeling of sadness and longing,
    That is not akin to pain,   10
And resembles sorrow only
    As the mist resembles the rain.

Come, read to me some poem,
    Some simple and heartfelt lay,
That shall soothe this restless feeling,   15
    And banish the thoughts of day.

Not from the grand old masters,
    Not from the bards sublime,
Whose distant footsteps echo
    Through the corridors of Time.   20

For, like strains of martial music,
    Their mighty thoughts suggest
Life's endless toil and endeavor;
    And to-night I long for rest.

Read from some humbler poet,   25
    Whose songs gushed from his heart,

As showers from the clouds of summer,
  Or tears from the eyelids start;

Who, through long days of labor,
  And nights devoid of ease,   30
Still heard in his soul the music
  Of wonderful melodies.

Such songs have power to quiet
  The restless pulse of care,
And come like the benediction   35
  That follows after prayer.

Then read from the treasured volume
  The poem of thy choice,
And lend to the rhyme of the poet
  The beauty of thy voice.   40

And the night shall be filled with music,
  And the cares, that infest the day,
Shall fold their tents, like the Arabs,
  And as silently steal away.

Explain the metaphors in stanza one.

Name some poems which you consider "mighty thoughts" of "bards sublime." Name some others which are songs of the "humbler poets."

Why is the evening the appropriate time for the reading of songs which "gushed from the heart"?

A LIMERICK

Anonymous

There was an old person of Fratton
Who would go to church with his hat on.
  "If I wake up," he said,
  "With my hat on my head,
I shall know that it hasn't been sat on."

TO CELIA

Ben Jonson

This famous love poem, perhaps the best known of all Elizabethan lyrics, has been set to familiar music. You doubtless have heard it sung many times. Now pay attention to the words.

> Drink to me only with thine eyes,
>   And I will pledge with mine;
> Or leave a kiss but in the cup,
>   And I'll not look for wine.
> The thirst that from the soul doth rise   5
>   Doth ask a drink divine;
> But might I of Jove's nectar sup,
>   I would not change for thine.
>
> I sent thee late a rosy wreath,
>   Not so much honoring thee   10
> As giving it a hope that there
>   It could not withered be;
> But thou thereon didst only breathe
>   And sent'st it back to me;
> Since when it grows, and smells, I swear,   15
>   Not of itself but thee!

If in this poem there are any lines which you do not understand, ask to have them explained. Why did the lover send his loved one a rosy wreath? Why did it not wither?

What do you think has made this lyric so famous for over three hundred years?

If, at the moment, you are in love, how does your reaction to this poem probably differ from that of a classmate who is fancy free?

JEANIE WITH THE LIGHT BROWN HAIR

Stephen Foster

Here is another love poem which in its musical setting is familiar to all. This one is by a nineteenth century American and may

148

be more to your taste than Jonson's Elizabethan lyric. Celia's sweetheart found joy in his love, but the heart of Jeanie's lover is full of sorrow and longing.

I dream of Jeanie with the light brown hair,
Borne, like a vapor, on the summer air;
I see her tripping where the bright streams play,
Happy as the daisies that dance on her way.

Many were the wild notes her merry voice would pour,   5
Many were the blithe birds that warbled them o'er:
Oh! I dream of Jeanie with the light brown hair,
Floating, like a vapor, on the summer air.

I long for Jeanie with the day-dawn smile,
Radiant in gladness, warm with winning guile;   10
I hear her melodies, like joys gone by,
Sighing round my heart o'er the fond hopes that die:—

Sighing like the wind and sobbing like the rain,—
Wailing for the lost one that comes not again:
Oh! I long for Jeanie, and my heart bows low,   15
Never more to find her where the bright waters flow.

How do you explain the popularity of this song? How do you yourself like it? How do you explain your personal reaction?
What metrical verse pattern is dominant? What are the characteristics of the stanza used?

IF I WERE KING
Justin Huntly McCarthy

This poem and the four which follow are five different comments on love, a subject of infinite variety to poets.

If I were king—ah, love, if I were king—
What tributary nations would I bring
To stoop before your sceptre and to swear
Allegiance to your lips and eyes and hair;
Beneath your feet what treasures I would fling:—   5
The stars should be your pearls upon a string,

149

The world a ruby for your finger ring,
And you should have the sun and moon to wear,
     If I were king.
Let these wild dreams and wilder words take wing,   10
Deep in the woods I hear a shepherd sing
A simple ballad, to a sylvan air,
Of love that ever finds your face more fair;
I could not give you any goodlier thing
     If I were king.   15

What makes the "wild words" of the lover "take wing"? Why is
the "simple ballad" a "goodlier thing" than the gifts in the "wild
dreams"? How do you react to the "wilder words"?

THE NIGHT HAS A THOUSAND EYES
Francis William Bourdillon

    The night has a thousand eyes,
      And the day but one;
    Yet the light of the bright world dies
      With the dying sun.

    The mind has a thousand eyes,   5
      And the heart but one;
    Yet the light of a whole life dies
      When love is done.

What are the "thousand eyes" of the night? of the mind? What is
the one light of the day? of the heart?
Do you consider this poem "wild words" or thoughtful comment?

DISDAIN RETURNED
Thomas Carew

    He that loves a rosy cheek,
      Or a coral lip admires,
    Or from starlike eyes doth seek

Fuel to maintain his fires;
As old Time makes these decay,   5
So his flames must waste away.

But a smooth and steadfast mind,
  Gentle thoughts, and calm desires,
Hearts with equal love combined,
  Kindle never-dying fires:—   10
Where these are not, I despise
Lovely cheeks or lips or eyes.

What fuels does the poet say produce only temporary flame; which
ones "kindle never-dying fires"? What fuel could you add to the lat-
ter?
Point out the metaphors in stanza one.

KO-KO'S SONG
from *The Mikado*
W. S. Gilbert

And now another lover's lament, this time a famous bit of
nonsense.

On a tree by a river a little tom-tit
  Sang "Willow, titwillow, titwillow!"
And I said to him, "Dicky-bird, why do you sit
  Singing 'Willow, titwillow, titwillow'?
Is it a weakness of intellect, birdie?" I cried,   5
"Or a rather tough worm in your little inside?"
With a shake of his poor little head he replied,
  "Oh, willow, titwillow, titwillow!"

He slapped at his chest, as he sat on that bough,
  Singing "Willow, titwillow, titwillow!"   10
And a cold perspiration bespangled his brow,
  Oh, willow, titwillow, titwillow!
He sobbed and he sighed, and a gurgle he gave,
Then he threw himself into the billowy wave,
And an echo arose from the suicide's grave—   15
  "Oh, willow, titwillow, titwillow!"

Now, I feel just as sure as I'm sure that my name
    Isn't Willow, titwillow, titwillow,
That 'twas blighted affection that made him exclaim,
    "Oh, willow, titwillow, titwillow!"   20
And if you remain callous and obdurate, I
Shall perish as he did, and you will know why,
Though I probably shall not exclaim as I die,
    "Oh, willow, titwillow, titwillow!"

LOVE IS LIKE A DIZZINESS

James Hogg

Love is like a dizziness,
It winna let a poor body
Gang about his bizziness.

SKY-WRITER

Vincent Starrett

    The young flier in this poem is telling himself—and you—
that if we go to great lengths to advertise a mere cigarette, how much
more fitting it is that we should let the world and skies know the
name of one loved: happy love *versus* a cigarette.

Today, while thousands stared with captured eyes,	a
And vaguely wondered how the thing was done,	b
Across the shifting billboard of the skies	a
There flashed an aeroplane that whirled and spun	b
Upward in some fantastical unrest,	c 5
Writing in smoke a flippant epithet,	d
As if to challenge Heaven itself to test	c
The virtues of that famous cigarette.	d
Much had I pondered how the world might learn	e
What wonder and what miracle was mine.	f 10
Lo, I have found a vehicle to burn	e

My boast of happiness from pole to line . . .   **f**
Harness your breeze, mad gods, and stand from under,   **g**
While I inscribe her name beside the thunder!   **g**

What other things besides the name of a loved one deserve, but seldom get, publicity? Name some honors or memorials which have been established for accomplishments long unrecognized (like "Mother of the Year").

In this sonnet what contrast in thought is made between the octet and the sestet?

GENTLE NAME

Selma Robinson

This little poem uses some unusual similes to express the poet's feeling about the name *Mary*. Note particularly her attempt to make you understand how she feels about the *sound* of this name by comparing it with the *sight* of a flame and the *smell* of a fern.

Mary is a gentle name
Like the sound of silver bells,
Like a blue and quiet flame,
Like country brooks and ferny smells;
A friendly, wistful name and airy—   5
Mary.

What is the key word in the poet's sound image of the name *Mary*? Did the things she chose for comparison help you to understand what she means by this key word? Which comparison did you find most helpful? Least helpful? What did the three adjectives in line 5 add to the poem as far as you were concerned?

Try to put into words your feeling about the sound of some name.

TO ALTHEA, FROM PRISON

Richard Lovelace

"Stone walls do not a prison make," sang Richard Lovelace over three hundred years ago, and today we still enjoy his famous lyric definition of true liberty.

When Love with unconfinèd wings
  Hovers within my gates,
And my divine Althea brings
  To whisper at the grates;
When I lie tangled in her hair   5
  And fettered to her eye,
The birds that wanton in the air
  Know no such liberty.

When flowing cups run swiftly round
  With no allaying Thames,   [The wine is   10
Our careless heads with roses bound,   not diluted
  Our hearts with loyal flames;   with water
When thirsty grief in wine we steep,   from the Thames.]
  When healths and draughts go free—
Fishes that tipple in the deep   15
  Know no such liberty.

When, like committed linnets, I   [Caged birds.]
  With shriller throat shall sing
The sweetness, mercy, majesty,
  And glories of my King;   [Charles I.] 20
When I shall voice aloud how good
  He is, how great should be,
Enlargèd winds, that curl the flood,
  Know no such liberty.

Stone walls do not a prison make,   25
  Nor iron bars a cage;
Minds innocent and quiet take
  That for an hermitage;
If I have freedom in my love
  And in my soul am free,   30
Angels alone, that soar above,
  Enjoy such liberty.

Name the three areas of freedom discussed in stanzas 1–3. Which
seems most important to you? Compare them with Franklin Roose-
velt's famous four freedoms: freedom of speech, freedom of worship,
freedom from want, freedom from fear. What is your own list?
  Commit the last stanza of the poem to memory.

SWEET SPRING IS YOUR

E. E. Cummings

One of the most musical of lyric poets writing today is E. E. Cummings, who lets his typographical idiosyncrasies chase some readers away.

It is spring, and love is in the air, everywhere—the birds, the sky, the sun, the trees and leaves, and the two hearts beating, singing of love!

Read the poem aloud, and don't worry too much about the exact meaning and structure of each line. Enjoy the joyful rhythm of the love song. (Where will you find a quatrain more lovely than the opening and closing stanza?)

"sweet spring is your
time is my time is our
time for springtime is lovetime
and viva sweet love"

(all the merry little birds are   5
flying in the floating in the
very spirits singing in
are winging in the blossoming)

lovers go and lovers come
awandering awondering   10
but any two are perfectly
alone there's nobody else alive

(such a sky and such a sun
i never knew and neither did you
and everybody never breathed   15
quite so many kinds of yes)

not a tree can count his leaves
each herself by opening
but shining who by thousands mean
only one amazing thing   20

(secretly adoring shyly
tiny winging darting floating

merry in the blossoming
always joyful selves are singing)

"sweet spring is your 25
time is my time is our
time for springtime is lovetime
and viva sweet love"

Well, did you like it? Good! "Viva sweet love!"

NUMBER 77 FROM 95 *Poems*
E. E. *Cummings*

i am a little church(no great cathedral)
far from the splendor and squalor of hurrying cities
—i do not worry if briefer days grow briefest,
i am not sorry when sun and rain make april

my life is the life of the reaper and the sower; 5
my prayers are prayers of earth's own clumsily striving
(finding and losing and laughing and crying)children
whose any sadness or joy is my grief or my gladness

around me surges a miracle of unceasing
birth and glory and death and resurrection: 10
over my sleeping self float flaming symbols
of hope,and i wake to a perfect patience of mountains

i am a little church(far from the frantic
world with its rapture and anguish)at peace with nature
—i do not worry if longer nights grow longest; 15
i am not sorry when silence becomes singing

winter by spring,i lift my diminutive spire to
merciful Him Whose only now is forever:
standing erect in the deathless truth of His presence
(welcoming humbly His light and proudly His darkness) 20

Here is another E. E. Cummings poem. This time a little country
church reveals its heart to us.
Do you think you would find satisfaction in saying a prayer in this

church? What are the details that would tend to bring you peace of mind?

What do you think E. E. Cummings is trying to express by his individualized punctuation and sentence structure? In what other arts do you find today similar rebellion against old, established forms?

EPIGRAM

(Engraved on the collar of a dog which I gave to His Royal Highness)

Alexander Pope

I am His Highness' dog at Kew;
Pray tell me, sir, whose dog are you?

A FEW SIGNS

Grantland Rice

To this hunter autumn means escape from the city to the "glory of the camp."

There's a north wind faintly calling, as the first dead leaves are
    falling,
Of a stretch of wooded country and our camp smoke, thin and
    blue;
And it speaks of quiet places, league on league from pallid faces,
Where the underbrush is silent till the big moose crashes through.

All my life gray fate has found me with the dizzy crowds around
    me,   5
Through the stadiums and subways ever wearily I tramp.
But when the north winds come to woo me there's a call that
    whispers to me
Of a solitude that beckons to the glory of the camp.

And at times along the low bank, far beneath the mountain's snow
    bank,
There are trout scales from a breakfast that no chef might ever
    know;   10

With the scent of bacon frying and the first ducks southward
   flying
From the bitter snarl of winter to a softer land below.

What do you find in autumn to make that season a rich annual ex-
perience?

THE SEA

Bryan Waller Procter

Here a man expresses his love for the sea. He was born on the
open sea, has lived on it as a sailor for fifty years, and hopes that
when death comes to him, it will be on "the wild, unbounded sea."

The sea! the sea! the open sea!
The blue, the fresh, the ever free!
Without a mark, without a bound,
It runneth the earth's wide regions round;
It plays with the clouds; it mocks the skies;   5
Or like a cradled creature lies.

I'm on the sea! I'm on the sea!
I am where I would ever be;
With the blue above, and the blue below,
And silence wheresoe'er I go;   10
If a storm should come and awake the deep,
What matter? *I* shall ride and sleep.

I love, O, how I love to ride
On the fierce, foaming, bursting tide,
When every mad wave drowns the moon,   15
Or whistles aloft his tempest tune,
And tells how goeth the world below,
And why the sou'west blasts do blow.

I never was on the dull, tame shore,
But I loved the great sea more and more,   20
And backwards flew to her billowy breast,
Like a bird that seeketh its mother's nest;
And a mother she was, and is, to me;
For I was born on the open sea!

158

The waves were white, and red the morn,   25
In the noisy hour when I was born;
And the whale it whistled, the porpoise rolled,
And the dolphins bared their backs of gold;
And never was heard such an outcry wild
As welcomed to life the ocean-child!   30

I've lived since then, in calm and strife,
Full fifty summers, a sailor's life,
With wealth to spend and a power to range,
But never have sought nor sighed for change;
And Death, whenever he comes to me,   35
Shall come on the wild, unbounded sea!

Did the sailor's enthusiasm seem sincere to you? Why, or why not?
If for any form of nature you have a love comparable to this sailor's
love for the sea, try to express this feeling in verse.

BREAK, BREAK, BREAK

Alfred Tennyson

This poem is a little masterpiece. Perhaps no one has more
perfectly stated the need for words to express grief than Tennyson
has done in this well-known poem. The sea can speak, the fisherman's
boy can shout, the sailor lad can sing, but the poet's tongue can find
no words to utter his longing for the loved one who has died.

Break, break, break,
    On thy cold gray stones, O Sea!
And I would that my tongue could utter
    The thoughts that arise in me.

O, well for the fisherman's boy,   5
    That he shouts with his sister at play!
O, well for the sailor lad,
    That he sings in his boat on the bay!

And the stately ships go on,
    To their haven under the hill;   10
But O for the touch of a vanished hand,
    And the sound of a voice that is still!

Break, break, break,
    At the foot of thy crags, O Sea!
But the tender grace of a day that is dead   15
    Will never come back to me.

In the first stanza, emphasize *my* and *me* to bring out the contrast between the sea and the poet.

Try reading the first line of stanzas 1 and 4 with a pause after each *break*. What effect does this reading have on the poem? What other effective uses of the pause are there in this poem?

What is added to the poem by the ships going on to their haven, in stanza 3? What do you understand by "tender grace" in stanza 4?

What other poems can you name which make an effort to utter grief in words?

O CAPTAIN! MY CAPTAIN!

Walt Whitman

Walt Whitman's famous elegy written upon the death of Abraham Lincoln is an indispensable part of our American literary heritage.

O Captain! my Captain! our fearful trip is done,
The ship has weather'd every rack, the prize we sought is won,
The port is near, the bells I hear, the people all exulting,
While follow eyes the steady keel, the vessel grim and daring;
        But O heart! heart! heart!   5
            O the bleeding drops of red,
                Where on the deck my Captain lies,
                    Fallen cold and dead.

O Captain! my Captain! rise up and hear the bells;
Rise up—for you the flag is flung—for you the bugle trills,   10
For you bouquets and ribbon'd wreaths—for you the shores
        a-crowding,
For you they call, the swaying mass, their eager faces turning;
        Here Captain! dear father!
            The arm beneath your head!
                It is some dream that on the deck,   15
                    You've fallen cold and dead.

My Captain does not answer, his lips are pale and still,
My father does not feel my arm, he has no pulse nor will,
The ship is anchor'd safe and sound, its voyage closed and done,
From fearful trip the victor ship comes in with object won;   20
    Exult O shores, and ring O bells!
      But I with mournful tread,
        Walk the deck my Captain lies,
      Fallen cold and dead.

What is the metaphor which continues throughout the poem? What two emotions are contrasted? What musical devices did you find effective?
What emotional progression is there from stanza to stanza?

THE TREES ARE DOWN

Charlotte Mew

The situation in this poem might have had a parallel in your own experience—that of witnessing trees, huge trees, cut down in your own yard or in your neighborhood. Perhaps you said in effect how quickly all this growing is put to an end. You had come to associate certain memories with these trees. Read to discover how Charlotte Mew was moved and what precise emotional response welled up within her.

    —and he cried with a loud voice:
  Hurt not the earth, neither the sea, nor the trees—
                (Revelation.)

They are cutting down the great plane-trees at the end of the
    gardens.
For days there has been the grate of the saw, the swish of the
    branches as they fall,
The crash of trunks, the rustle of trodden leaves,
With the "Whoops" and the "Whoas," the loud common talk, the
    loud common laughs of the men, above it all.

I remember one evening of a long past Spring   5
Turning in at a gate, getting out of a cart, and finding a large
    dead rat in the mud of the drive.

I remember thinking: alive or dead, a rat was a god-forsaken
thing,
But at least, in May, that even a rat should be alive.

The week's work here is as good as done. There is just one bough
On the roped bole, in the fine grey rain,   10
Green and high
And lonely against the sky.
(Down now!—)
And but for that,
If an old dead rat   15
Did once, for a moment, unmake the Spring, I might never have
thought of him again.

It is not for a moment the Spring is unmade to-day;
These were great trees, it was in them from root to stem:
When the men with the "Whoops" and the "Whoas" have carted
the whole of the whispering loveliness away
Half the Spring, for me, will have gone with them.   20

It is going now, and my heart has been struck with the hearts of
the planes;
Half my life it has beat with these, in the sun, in the rains,
In the March wind, the May breeze,
In the great gales that came over to them across the roofs from the
great seas.
There was only a quiet rain when they were dying;   25
They must have heard the sparrows flying,
And the small creeping creatures in the earth where they were
lying—
But I, all day, I heard an angel crying:
"Hurt not the trees."

What is the connection between the trees and the dead rat?
How does the emotion in this poem differ from that in "Woodman,
Spare That Tree"?

JAZZ FANTASIA

Carl Sandburg

To catch in words the spirit of a jazz "fantasia" (an im-
provised composition, unrestricted by set form) is a difficult assign-
ment. See how well you think Carl Sandburg has succeeded.

Drum on your drums, batter on your banjos, sob on the long cool
winding saxophones. Go to it, O jazzmen.

Sling your knuckles on the bottoms of the happy tin pans, let your
trombones ooze, and go husha-husha-hush with the slippery
sandpaper.

Moan like an autumn wind high in the lonesome treetops, moan
soft like you wanted somebody terrible, cry like a racing car
slipping away from a motorcycle-cop, bang-bang! you jazz-
men, bang altogether drums, traps, banjos, horns, tin cans—
make two people fight on the top of a stairway and scratch
each other's eyes in a clinch tumbling down the stairs.

Can the rough stuff . . . Now a Mississippi steamboat pushes up
the night river with a hoo-hoo-hoo-oo . . . and the green
lanterns calling to the high soft stars . . . a red moon rides
on the humps of the low river hills. . . . Go to it, O jazzmen.

What are some particularly effective words? images? comparisons?
examples of onomatopoeia?
How would you defend the use of sub-standard English?
By what definition of poetry can you call this selection a poem?

CROSSING

Philip Booth

This poem is a good example of how a common, even hum-
drum, experience can through poetry be made fun. Haven't you had
to sit and sit until a freight train went by? To while away the tedium
you counted or read the names on the boxcars. Through his skill in
language, Philip Booth makes us relive that experience with fun.

STOP   LOOK   LISTEN
as gate stripes swing down,
count the cars hauling distance
upgrade through town:
warning whistle, bell clang,   5
engine eating steam,
engineer waving,
a fast-freight dream;
B. & M. boxcar,
boxcar again,   10
Frisco gondola,
eight-nine-ten,
Erie and Wabash,
Seaboard, U.P.,
Pennsy tank car,   15
twenty-two, three,
Phoebe Snow, B. & O.,
thirty-four, five,
Santa Fe cattle
shipped alive,   20
red cars, yellow cars,
orange cars, black,
Youngstown steel
down to Mobile
on Rock Island track,   25
fifty-nine, sixty,
hoppers of coke,
Anaconda copper,
hotbox smoke,
eighty-eight,   30
red-ball freight,
Rio Grande,
Nickel Plate,
Hiawatha,
Lackawanna,   35
rolling fast
and loose,
ninety-seven,

coal car,
boxcar,   40
CABOOSE!

State in one sentence the progression that takes place within the
poem.
What would have been the effect if the poet had employed cou-
plets? What rime does the poet use?
Recall this poem the next time you have to wait for a freight train.
Compare and contrast the two experiences.

TELE-NEWS BLUES

Peter Dufault

This poet imagines himself at a teletype machine, improvising
a blues song—melancholy in tone and employing much repetition.

Listen to the listen to the
tel to the tel to the tel tel
to the tel tel tel tel tel
of the teletype machine
as it ham as it ham ham   5
as it hammer hammer hammers
as it stammers as it stammers
with the new with the new news
with the new news news with the news
I refuse   10
I refuse to peruse
tho I lose lose lose
the advantage that accrues
from a knowledge of the news—
to peruse   15
the catastrophes they choose
to disseminate as news
I am more
I am MORE MORE MORE
I am more   20
constituted to deplore
the eternal tick tick

of the journal tick tick
of the journalistic tick
of accuse of abuse   25
of expose diagnose
of the
KILL KILL KILL KILL KILL
Yet I yet
Yet I yet yet   30
Yet (I wonder what the dirt is)
yet I listen listen
listen to the listen to the
listen to the zzz y zzz y zzz
to the zzz y CORRECTION   35
I peruse
to the zzz
to the zzz y zzz
all the way to the y
to the zzz zzz   40
to the zzz y
30 30 THIRTIES

What is your understanding of and emotional response to this
poem? What meaning is communicated to you? Try singing this poem.
Improvise. How does the rhythm of the poem help you?

SNEEZING

Leigh Hunt

What a moment, what a doubt!
All my nose is inside out,—
All my thrilling, tickling caustic,
Pyramid rhinocerostic,
   Wants to sneeze and cannot do it!   5
How it yearns me, thrills me, stings me,
How with rapturous torment wrings me!
   Now says, "Sneeze, you fool,—get through it."
Shee—shee—oh! 'tis most del—ishi—

Ishi—ishi—most del—ishi!
(Hang it, I shall sneeze till spring!)
Snuff is a delicious thing.

IRON-WIND DANCES

from "Thunderstorms"

Lew Sarett

The rhythm of the war-dance makes the emotional impact of this poem terrifyingly real. Read it aloud.

Over and under
The shaking sky,
The war-drums thunder
When I dance by!—
Ho! a warrior proud,   5
I dance on a cloud,
For my ax shall feel
The enemy reel;
My heart shall thrill
To a bloody kill,—   10
Ten Sioux dead
Split open of head!—
Look! to the West!—
The sky-line drips,—
Blood from the breast!   15
Blood from the lips!
Ho! when I dance by,
The war-drums thunder
Over and under
The shaking sky.   20
Beat, beat on the drums,
For the Thunderbird comes.
Wuh!
Wuh!

WHAT THE HYENA SAID

Vachel Lindsay

This poem transports you to a realm of fantasy—of grim
fantasy. The poet intends to make you feel uncomfortable. A dead
moon and Moon-Worms and a dead earth await you.

> The moon is but a golden skull,
> She mounts the heavens now,
> And Moon-Worms, mighty Moon-Worms
> Are wreathed around her brow.
>
> The Moon-Worms are a doughty race: 5
> They eat her gray and golden face.
> Her eye-sockets dead, and molding head:
> These caverns are their dwelling-place.
>
> The Moon-Worms, serpents of the skies,
> From the great hollows of her eyes   10
> Behold all souls, and they are wise:
> With tiny, keen and icy eyes,
> Behold how each man sins and dies.
>
> When Earth in gold-corruption lies
> Long dead, the moon-worm butterflies   15
> On cyclone wings will reach this place—
> Yea, rear their brood on earth's dead face.

Why is it sometimes valuable for a person to be made uncom-
fortable? What criticism of life on earth did you find in this poem?
What do you feel was the emotional state of the poet when he
wrote this poem? What emotion did the poem arouse in you?

BEAT! BEAT! DRUMS!

Walt Whitman

The drums are those of war, war giving its own alarm, calling
all men to battle, without pity or remorse. Beneath the harsh tone in
which the subject is presented beats a heart filled with pity but
also an awareness of war's ironies.

Beat! beat! drums!—blow! bugles! blow!
Through the windows—through doors—burst like a ruthless force,
Into the solemn church, and scatter the congregation,
Into the school where the scholar is studying;
Leave not the bridegroom quiet—no happiness must he have now
    with his bride,   5
Nor the peaceful farmer any peace, ploughing his field or gather-
    ing his grain,
So fierce you whirr and pound you drums—so shrill you bugles
    blow.

Beat! beat! drums!—blow! bugles! blow!
Over the traffic of cities—over the rumble of wheels in the streets;
Are beds prepared for sleepers at night in the houses? no sleepers
    must sleep in those beds,   10
No bargainers' bargains by day—no brokers or speculators—
    would they continue?
Would the talkers be talking? would the singer attempt to sing?
Would the lawyer rise in the court to state his case before the
    judge?
Then rattle quicker, heavier drums—you bugles wilder blow.

Beat! beat! drums!—blow! bugles! blow!   15
Make no parley—stop for no expostulation,
Mind not the timid—mind not the weeper or prayer,
Mind not the old man beseeching the young man,
Let not the child's voice be heard, nor the mother's entreaties,
Make even the trestles to shake the dead where they lie awaiting
    the hearses,   20
So strong you thump O terrible drums—so loud you bugles blow.

    What emotional and thought progression is found in the poem?
    From whom do the cries of the opposition come?

GOD'S WORLD

Edna St. Vincent Millay

    If you have ever felt that autumn color was almost too beauti-
ful to be borne, you will find expression for your emotion in this pas-
sionate outburst by Edna Millay.

O world, I cannot hold thee close enough!	a
Thy winds, thy wide grey skies!	b
Thy mists that roll and rise!	b
Thy woods, this autumn day, that ache and sag	c
And all but cry with color! That gaunt crag	c 5
To crush! To lift the lean of that black bluff!	a
World, World, I cannot get thee close enough!	a
Long have I known a glory in it all,	a
But never knew I this;	b
Here such a passion is	b 10
As stretcheth me apart. Lord, I do fear	c
Thou'st made the world too beautiful this year.	c
My soul is all but out of me,—let fall	a
No burning leaf; prithee, let no bird call.	a

Point out a sentence containing two excellent bits of alliteration. Compare this poem with "Autumn Tints." Which do you prefer? Why?

What is the stanzaic pattern? (Check the number of lines, the meter of each line, and the rime scheme.)

This is a good poem to commit to memory.

AUTUMN TINTS

Mathilde Blind

Many, many poems have been written about autumn. You can guess from the title that the imagery in this poem will be largely visual. Let the specific details unite to form the total picture; create a word-painting as you read along from stanza to stanza.

Coral-colored yew-berries
Strew the garden ways,
Hollyhocks and sunflowers
Make a dazzling blaze
In these latter days.   5

Marigolds by cottage doors
Flaunt their golden pride,
Crimson-punctured bramble leaves

Dapple far and wide
The green mountain-side.   10

Far away, on hilly slopes
Where fleet rivulets run,
Miles on miles of tangled fern,
Burnished by the sun,
Glow a copper dun.   15

For the year that's on the wane,
Gathering all its fire,
Flares up through the kindling world
As, ere they expire,
Flames leap high and higher.   20

How many of the details have been experienced by you? What is
the meaning of "fire" in the last stanza?

What is the emotional tone of the poem?

Could you take this poem to a certain kind of competent painter
and have him use it as the basis for a painting? (If you have any
talent along these lines, try it yourself.) On what grounds might other
painters refuse such a commission?

THE COIN

Sara Teasdale

That the "heart's treasury" of lovely memories is beyond price
is neatly stated in this short bit of verse.

Into my heart's treasury
I slipped a coin
That time cannot take
Nor a thief purloin—
Oh, better than the minting   5
Of a gold-crowned king
Is the safe-kept memory
Of a lovely thing.

Compare this poem with "I Wandered Lonely as a Cloud" (p. 77).
Which poem appeals more to you? Which would you prefer to memo-
rize?

What do you think is the meaning of *safe-kept* in line 7? What con-
sistency is maintained in the imagery if *safe* is a noun?

171

A BALLADE-CATALOGUE OF LOVELY THINGS

Richard Le Gallienne

This poem is interesting for two reasons: it presents a discriminating list of "lovely things to hold in memory against evil days," and it is written in the form of a ballade.

I would make a list against the evil days
　Of lovely things to hold in memory:
First I set down my lady's lovely face,
　For earth has no such lovely thing as she;
　And next I add, to bear her company,　　　　　　5
The great-eyed virgin star that morning brings;
　Then the wild-rose upon its little tree—
So runs my catalogue of lovely things.

The enchanted dogwood, with its ivory trays,
　The water-lily in its sanctuary　　　　　　　　10
Of reeded pools, and dew-drenched lilac sprays;
　For these, of all fair flowers, the fairest be;
　Next write I down the great name of the sea,
Lonely in its greatness as the names of kings;
　Then the young moon that hath us all in fee—　　15
So runs my catalogue of lovely things.

Imperial sunsets that in crimson blaze
　Along the hills, and fairer still to me,
The fireflies dancing in a netted maze
　Woven of twilight and tranquility;　　　　　　20
　Shakespeare and Virgil, their high poesy;
Then a great ship, splendid with snowy wings,
　Voyaging on into eternity—
So runs my catalogue of lovely things.

Envoy

Prince, not the gold bars of thy treasury,　　　　25
　Not all thy jewelled sceptres, crowns and rings,

Are worth the honeycomb of the wild bee—
So runs my catalogue of lovely things.

The *ballade* (not to be confused with the ballad) is a popular French verse form. The details of the ballade vary from poet to poet, but the constant elements seem to be a refrain, an envoy, and no more than three rimes.

In Mr. Le Gallienne's ballade, what is the refrain? What is the rime scheme? Point out examples of assonance.

Which ones of Mr. Le Gallienne's "lovely things" appealed to you? Which ones had no appeal? What would you like to add? Which list do you prefer, this one or Miss Teasdale's in "Barter" (p. 68)?

ALADDIN THROWS AWAY HIS LAMP

Elias Lieberman

The scientific wonders of our modern world convince Aladdin that he needs no magic lamp to call up jinns. He tells us about it in the form of a sonnet.

A zooming overhead . . . and steel-framed birds
Swoop by, intent on missions far away;
Within my room a cabinet yields words,
Sings, plays, and entertains me night or day.
To signal bells a sentiment arrives   5
From distant friends, I pluck a wire and talk;
A motor energizes wheels, contrives
A magic car for those who will not walk.
I turn a faucet . . . cooling waters spout
And gladden throats that may be parched for thirst;   10
I press a button . . . brilliant light pours out
Through globes of glass . . . the darkness flees, accursed.
I need no lamp in which a jinn may dwell;
My commonplace outdoes his miracle.

Name the miraculous details of Aladdin's "commonplace." What ones would you have chosen? Which would you prefer, a ride on a jet plane or on a magic carpet? Why?

IT ISN'T THE COUGH
Anonymous

It isn't the cough
That carries you off;
It's the coffin
They carry you off in.

OTHERWISE
Aileen Fisher

"Why?" and "How?" are the ever-present questions of child-hood. Even as adults, we never find all the answers. It would be a bad day when we lost all our child-like wonder at the "magic" of the universe.

There must be magic:
Otherwise,
How could day turn to night?
And how could sailboats,
Otherwise,   5
Go sailing out of sight?
And how could peanuts,
Otherwise,
Be covered up so tight?

Name the three things which caused this poet to declare whimsi-cally that "there must be magic." What things cause a similar reaction in you?

THE LIGHTNING IS A YELLOW FORK
Emily Dickinson

Emily Dickinson has a way of suggesting to our imaginations novel and weird observations. Her way of seeing startles us into at-tentiveness and alertness in seeing anew the everyday world about us.

The lightning is a yellow fork
From tables in the sky
By inadvertent fingers dropped,
The awful cutlery

Of mansions never quite disclosed   5
And never quite concealed,
The apparatus of the dark
To ignorance revealed.

Explain the details of the metaphor. Select another common thing like lightning and write a brief unusual metaphor through which your reader will see as he has not seen before.

A PITCHER OF MIGNONETTE

H. C. Bunner

The mignonette is a long-stemmed garden annual having clusters of fragrant greenish white flowers. In this little poem a bouquet of these comes to stand for more than just flowers. The object or image becomes a symbol.

A pitcher of mignonette
In a tenement's highest casement,—
Queer sort of flower-pot—yet
That pitcher of mignonette
Is a garden in heaven set,   5
To the little sick child in the basement—
The pitcher of mignonette,
In a tenement's highest casement.

What is the name for poems of this form?
What does the pitcher of mignonette become a symbol of?

A LIMERICK

Anonymous

There was a young man from Trinity,
Who solved the square root of infinity.
While counting the digits,
He was seized by the fidgets,
Dropped science, and took up divinity.

THE RAIN

William H. Davies

All of us have experienced rain many times, and it may be responsible for instilling in us various emotional states. In this poem we feel the beneficent effect and the beauty in nature rain is responsible for. The poem conveys the glory of the commonplace.

I hear leaves drinking Rain,
    I hear rich leaves on top
Giving the poor beneath
    Drop after drop;
'Tis a sweet noise to hear   5
These green leaves drinking near.

And when the Sun comes out,
    After this rain shall stop,
A wondrous Light will fill
    Each dark, round drop;   10
I hope the Sun shines bright;
'Twill be a lovely sight.

To what senses does the imagery appeal?
In your interpretation is there any reason for the poet's capitalizing Rain, Sun, and Light?
What is the rime scheme of the stanza? Notice how the poet, through the use of run-on lines, does not let the rime bother his thought.

MANHATTAN SKYLINE

Eugene M. Kayden

Perhaps too frequently the drab and crude aspects of a big city are unduly emphasized. In this triolet the poet alerts us to the beauty that exists in a city's architecture and the play of light upon it.

As blossoms white, bricks quiver in light,
As blossoms white of the apple:
Wing on wing, sky-going, poised for a flight,
As blossoms white, bricks quiver in light.

Walls rise to the sky from the pit of night   5
As tapers alight in a chapel. . . .
As blossoms white, bricks quiver in light,
As blossoms white of the apple.

To what two things are the bricks in the light compared? Which simile did you find the more helpful in creating the image in your own mind?
Be sure you understand the third line.

THE DONKEY

G. K. Chesterton

To Mr. Chesterton the sight of a donkey creates thoughts and feelings much deeper and more important than the all too common derision for this "tattered outlaw of the earth."

When fishes flew and forests walked
    And figs grew upon thorn,
Some moment when the moon was blood,
    Then surely I was born;

With monstrous head and sickening cry   5
    And ears like errant wings,
The devil's walking parody
    On all four-footed things.

The tattered outlaw of the earth,
    Of ancient crooked will;   10
Starve, scourge, deride me: I am dumb,
    I keep my secret still.

Fools! For I also had my hour;
    One far fierce hour and sweet:
There was a shout about my ears,   15
    And palms before my feet.

Which of the phrases used to describe or characterize the donkey did you find most appropriate? What are "errant wings"? (What is the difference in meaning between *errant* and *arrant?*)
If you can think of some other animal—perhaps a specific one, like your dog or a friend's parakeet—or a seemingly insignificant person, or even a mere object like a piece of furniture, which "had its hour," tell the class about that hour.

THE EXAMPLE

William H. Davies

Share with this poet his delight in seeing beauty in the common things about us.

Here's an example from
A Butterfly;
That on a rough, hard rock
Happy can lie;
Friendless and all alone   5
On this unsweetened stone.

Now let my bed be hard,
No care take I;
I'll make my joy like this
Small Butterfly;   10
Whose happy heart has power
To make a stone a flower.

Explain the metaphor in the last line. From your own experience give some examples of beauty that you have found in the commonplace.

ON A FLY DRINKING OUT OF HIS CUP

William Oldys

Poets view commonplace things and events with imagination and thoughtfulness. A fly drinking out of his cup causes this poet no irritation; instead he expresses a fellow feeling with the fly, trying to make the most of a life all too short for both fly and man.

Busy, curious, thirsty fly!
Drink with me and drink as I:
Freely welcome to my cup,
Couldst thou sip and sip it up:
Make the most of life you may,   5
Life is short and wears away.

Both alike are mine and thine
Hastening quick to their decline:
Thine's a summer, mine's no more,
Though repeated to threescore.   10
Threescore summers, when they're gone,
Will appear as short as one!

What other poem do you know that suggests we should "make the
most of life"? (See p. 69.)

What do you think would be your reaction to a fly drinking out of
your cup—or glass? If any insect or small animal has ever inspired
you to a bit of philosophizing, tell the class about it. Ask your teacher
to read you Robert Burns's "To a Louse."

THE SPIDER

Robert P. Tristram Coffin

Here is another insect as seen through the eyes and mind of
a poet.

With six small diamonds for his eyes
He walks upon the Summer skies,
Drawing from his silken blouse
The lacework of his dwelling house.

He lays his staircase as he goes   5
Under his eight thoughtful toes
And grows with the concentric flower
Of his shadowless, thin bower.

His back legs are a pair of hands,
They can spindle out the strands   10
Of a thread that is so small
It stops the sunlight not at all.

He spins himself to threads of dew
Which will harden soon into
Lines that cut like slender knives   15
Across the insects' airy lives.

179

He makes no motion but is right,
He spreads out his appetite
Into a network, twist on twist,
This little ancient scientist. 20

He does not know he is unkind,
He has a jewel for a mind
And logic deadly as dry bone,
This small son of Euclid's own.

List the items which show that Mr. Coffin was a careful observer.
Point out a comparison which pleased you. Is it a simile, or a meta-
phor?
Restate line one of stanza five in your own words.
What do you think Mr. Coffin means by the last stanza? Why is it
appropriate to call a spider "this small son of Euclid's own"?

AT THE AQUARIUM

Max Eastman

This poem requires a little thinking and participation on your
part. You are both the people looking at the fish in their cages, so to
speak, out of their natural habitat, and you are also the fish looking
at the people. The tone is one of mockery. Are the aims and purposes
of men sometimes any more clearly stated and defined than that of the
aimless motions of the fish?

Serene the silver fishes glide,
Stern-lipped, and pale, and wonder-eyed!
As, through the aged deeps of ocean,
They glide with wan and wavy motion.
They have no pathway where they go, 5
They flow like water to and fro,
They watch with never-winking eyes,
They watch with staring, cold surprise,
The level people in the air,
The people peering, peering there: 10
Who wander also to and fro,
And know not why or where they go,
Yet have a wonder in their eyes,
Sometimes a pale and cold surprise.

What general characterization is given to the fish?
How does the title add additional irony to the poem?
Explain the meaning of line 9; of line 14.
Prove that this fourteen-line poem is not a sonnet.

A NARROW FELLOW IN THE GRASS

Emily Dickinson

Each person has a way of reacting to things like bats, owls, and snakes. This poem is about the last—in the singular, as if one at a time is sufficient.

A narrow fellow in the grass
Occasionally rides;
You may have met him,—did you not?
His notice sudden is.

The grass divides as with a comb,   5
A spotted shaft is seen;
And then it closes at your feet
And opens further on.

He likes a boggy acre,
A floor too cool for corn.   10
Yet when a child, and barefoot,
I more than once, at morn,

Have passed, I thought, a whiplash
Unbraiding in the sun,—
When, stooping to secure it,   15
It wrinkled, and was gone.

Several of nature's people
I know, and they know me;
I feel for them a transport
Of cordiality;   20

But never met this fellow,
Attended or alone,
Without a tighter breathing,
And zero at the bone.

What was your emotional response to this poem?
What figures of speech do you find?
What is your reaction to snakes? Why do some people feel revulsion while others feel "a transport of cordiality"?

THE DIFFERENCE

Anonymous

'Twixt optimist and pessimist
    The difference is droll;
The optimist sees the doughnut;
    The pessimist sees the hole.

FERRY RIDE

Selma Robinson

Have you ever felt happy in the magic of spring and then had your joy killed for some reason which you couldn't quite explain to yourself? If you have, you will understand this New York girl, whose lovely day was spoiled, though she didn't know just why.

I hailed the bus and I went for a ride
And I rode on top and not inside
As I'd done on every other day:
The air was so sweet and the city so gay
The sun was so hot and the air so mellow   5
And the shops were bursting with green and yellow.

The shops were the brightest I'd ever seen—
Full of yellow and pink and green,
Yellow in this and green in that,
A dress or a 'kerchief, a tie or a hat,   10
And I wanted to dance and I wanted to sing
And I bought a flower because it was spring.

Then I walked across a dozen blocks
Until I came to the river docks.
Oh, the sky was so soft and the ships were so white   15
That I wanted to sail and I wanted to fly
And I didn't know why—and I *don't* know why.

The day was so good and the water so sunny
I would have sailed, if I'd had the money,
I didn't know how and I didn't know where.   20
But I had enough for a ferry fare
To take me to Jersey and back again;
(Good-bye to Norway, good-bye to Spain!)

The boat was old and the freight it ferried
Was old enough to be dead and buried;   25
Old, old horses in tottering rows,
Three old women who sat like crows
And a limping dog and a sleeping man
And an evil smell like a refuse can.

I don't know why—but the spell was broken   30
And by the time we had left Hoboken
The day grew drab and the wind blew chilly,
Something had changed, and I felt so silly
Holding a flower and wanting to cry.
And I didn't know why—and I don't know why.   35

Would you call this poem narrative or lyric?
Did you yourself feel the two emotions as the poet described them?
How helpful did you find the rhythm and rime in expressing them?

THE OLD SWIMMER

Christopher Morley

The old swimmer is not a swimmer now, as the first and last
stanzas tell. He is still enticed by the sea, but leaves the swimming
up to others. In the intervening stanzas the man recalls the sensuous
delights he once found in swimming, particularly in the days of his
youth.

I often wander on the beach
  Where once, so brown of limb,
The biting air, the roaring surf
  Summoned me to swim.

I see my old abundant youth   5
  Where combers lean and spill,

And though I taste the foam no more
  Other swimmers will.

Oh, good exultant strength to meet
  The arching wall of green,   10
To break the crystal, swirl, emerge
  Dripping, taut, and clean.

To climb the moving hilly blue,
  To dive in ecstasy
And feel the salty chill embrace   15
  Arm and rib and knee.

What brave and vanished laughter then
  And tingling thighs to run,
What warm and comfortable sands
  Dreaming in the sun.   20

The crumbling water spreads in snow,
  The surf is hissing still,
. And though I kiss the salt no more,
  Other swimmers will.

How does your own experience as a swimmer testify to the truth
of the old swimmer's delights? What various images are called to
your mind by the imagery? To what senses do these appeal?
  In the third, fourth, and fifth stanzas, the poet uses sentence frag-
ments. In your opinion, what does this device help to communicate?
  Write a poem in which you become lyrical about the joys of swim-
ming.

THE LITTLE MAN WHO WASN'T THERE
Hughes Mearns

As I was going up the stair
  I met a man who wasn't there!
He wasn't there again today!
  I wish, I *wish* he'd stay away!

SIX NUNS IN THE SNOW

Phyllis McGinley

This poem is an excellent example of the way lyric poets
open our eyes to the significance and beauty of things which have
formerly appeared to us as commonplace and of no special interest.
This delightful image of the six nuns will remain forever in your
mind if you read this poem carefully. (Note that it is a *moving* pic-
ture: don't miss the "placid tread.")

Beautifully, now, they walk among these new
petals the snow shook down—
identical figures, going two by two,
each in a black gown.

With what a placid tread, what definite,   5
calm impulse each proceeds,
two by two, black on bewildering white,
swinging her long beads;

an absolute six, taking their candid way
undazzled by this whiteness,   10
who have grown used to walking without dismay
amid incredible brightness.

What is the meaning of the last two lines? What is meant by the
"definite, calm impulse"?

THUNDERSTORMS

William H. Davies

The thunderstorms in this poem are not the ones you and I
usually think of. They are figurative, taking place in the mind.

My mind has thunderstorms,
    That brood for heavy hours:
Until they rain me words,
    My thoughts are drooping flowers
And sulking, silent birds.   5

185

Yet come, dark thunderstorms,
And brood your heavy hours;
For when you rain me words,
My thoughts are dancing flowers
And joyful singing birds.   10

Explain each of the metaphors. Tell whether or not you consider these metaphors to be symbols.

Exactly what changes the poet's thoughts from "sulky, silent birds" to "joyful singing birds"? (Did you ever experience such a transformation when trying to write a theme?)

THE BARE ARMS OF TREES
John Tagliabue

Here is the poetic imagination superbly alert. The bare branches of trees stir up in this poet's mind thoughts of the barrenness and loneliness of some persons' lives.

Sometimes when I see the bare arms of trees in the evening
I think of men who have died without love,
Of desolation and space between branch and branch,
I think of immovable whiteness and lean coldness and fear
And the terrible longing between people stretched apart as these
    branches   5
And the cold space between.
I think of the vastness and courage between this step and that
    step
Of the yearning and fear of the meeting, of the terrible desire
    held apart.
I think of the ocean of longing that moves between land and land
And between people, the space and ocean.   10
The bare arms of the trees are immovable, without the play of
    leaves, without the sound of wind;
I think of the unseen and the unknown thoughts that exist be-
    tween tree and tree
As I pass these things in the evening, as I walk.

Why do the trees make the poet think of "men who have died without love"? What caused the lack in these men's lives?

If this poem failed to move you, what is probably the reason?

JUNK

Richard Wilbur

To express his contempt for the shoddy workmanship which produced the junk now discarded and awaiting the trash-man's truck, Richard Wilbur has followed faithfully the Anglo-Saxon verse form. Read the poem aloud, giving full play to the alliteration and the pauses—and the thought—and the emotion.

An axe angles from my neighbor's ashcan;
It is hell's handiwork, the wood not hickory
The flow of the grain not faithfully followed.
The shivered shaft rises from a shellheap
Of plastic playthings, paper plates,   5
And the sheer shards of shattered tumblers
That were not annealed for the time needful.
At the same curbside, a cast-off cabinet
Of wavily-warped unseasoned wood
Waits to be trundled in the trash-man's truck.   10
Haul them off! Hide them! The heart winces
For junk and gimcrack, for jerrybuilt things
And the men who make them for a little money,
Bartering pride like the bought boxer
Who pulls his punches, or the paid-off jockey   15
Who in the home stretch holds in his horse.
Yet the things themselves in thoughtless honor
Have kept composure, like the captives who would not
Talk under torture. Tossed from a tailgate
Where the dump displays its random dolmens,   20
Its black barrows and blazing valleys,
They shall waste in the weather toward what they were.
The sun shall glory in the glitter of glass-chips,
Foreseeing the salvage of the prisoned sand,
And the blistering paint peel off in patches,   25
That the good grain be discovered again.
Then burnt, bulldozed, they shall be buried
To the depth of diamonds, in the making dark

Where halt Hephaestus   keeps his hammer
And Wayland's work   is worn away.   30

20. *dolmens:* mounds
29. *Hephaestus:* Greek god of fire and metal work (Roman god Vulcan)
30. *Wayland:* smith of English and Teutonic legend (called Weland by
Deor—see p. 222)

What was wrong with each item mentioned as "junk"? To whom
does Mr. Wilbur compare the men who made them? To whom does
he compare the things themselves? Explain why you approve, or dis-
approve, of these comparisons. What is the final fate of these pieces
of junk? Do you consider this fate tragedy, or triumph?

MARTIN

Joyce Kilmer

Martin, scorned by many as a failure while alive, is remem-
bered by this poet as a success.

> When I am tired of earnest men,
>   Intense and keen and sharp and clever,
> Pursuing fame with brush or pen
>   Or counting metal disks forever,
> Then from the halls of shadowland   5
>   Beyond the trackless purple sea
> Old Martin's ghost comes back to stand
>   Beside my desk and talk to me.
>
> Still on his delicate pale face
>   A quizzical thin smile is showing,   10
> His cheeks are wrinkled like fine lace,
>   His kind blue eyes are gay and glowing.
> He wears a brilliant-hued cravat,
>   A suit to match his soft gray hair,
> A rakish stick, a knowing hat,   15
>   A manner blithe and debonair.
>
> How good, that he who always knew
>   That being lovely was a duty,
> Should have gold halls to wander through
>   And should himself inhabit beauty.   20

How like his old unselfish way
   To leave those halls of splendid mirth
And comfort those condemned to stay
   Upon the bleak and sombre earth.

Some people ask: What cruel chance   25
   Made Martin's life so sad a story?
Martin? Why, he exhaled romance
   And wore an overcoat of glory.
A fleck of sunlight in the street,
   A horse, a book, a girl who smiled,—   30
Such visions made each moment sweet
   For this receptive, ancient child.

Because it was old Martin's lot
   To be, not make, a decoration,
Shall we then scorn him, having not   35
   His genius of appreciation?
Rich joy and love he got and gave;
   His heart was merry as his dress.
Pile laurel wreaths upon his grave
   Who did not gain, but was, success.   40

What vocations are mentioned as those of "earnest men" who,
though "keen and sharp and clever," are sometimes too "intense"?
   Why is the simile in line 11 exceptionally good? What is a "blithe
and debonair" manner?
   Point out some particularly well-phrased ideas; e.g., "being lovely
was a duty."
   Do you think you would have liked Martin? Give your reasons.

THE PERFECT REACTIONARY

Hughes Mearns

As I was sitting in my chair
I *knew* the bottom wasn't there,
Nor legs nor back, but I *just sat,*
Ignoring little things like that.

UNCLE BING

Vincent Starrett

Excuses are frequently the frailties of human beings. Sometimes only an experience like the one in this poem can jar us into awareness of shortcomings that exist within us, especially in our attitudes toward others.

At first it was too hot, and then too wet,
And then too cold to visit Uncle Bing.
We cursed the summer, cursed the fall, and yet
Found cause to curse the winter and the spring;
And when again spring rolled around, the rain   5
Was quite as wet as usual, and we
Found summer much too close and hot again
To drag us any place except the sea.

The upshot was we never drove the nine
Long weary miles to Uncle Bingham's farm,   10
Until one day, in weather fit for swine,
We made the trip in haste, in some alarm.
It seemed a shame that Uncle Bing should die
Before we had a chance to say good-bye.

What really kept the people from visiting Uncle Bing? Why do you feel they even bothered to go when they did? How do you interpret the closing couplet? What details of the poem do you consider satirical?

How would you classify the rime scheme in this sonnet? (See p. 62.)

THE WRESTLER

Stefan George

Translated by David Luke

Occasionally a poet, by merely presenting us a picture of a person, tells us much of that person's history and character—and also some truths of human nature. "The Wrestler" is such a poem.

His arm—a wonder and an admiration—
He rests on his right hip, and the sun plays
On his strong limbs and on the laurel wreath
That crowns his brow; slowly the cheering sweeps
The ranks of people as he passes by   5
Along the street all strewn with greenery.
The women lift their children high and teach them
How to cry out his name in acclamation
And hold palm branches out to him in homage.
He walks full-footed as the lion walks,   10
Unsmiling, after many fameless years
Now nation-honored, and he does not see
The vast rejoicing crowd, or even notice
His parents' pride head high among them all.

How does the wrestler feel about all the honor he is receiving?
What general truths of human nature does he exemplify?

THE TRAVEL BUREAU

Ruth Comfort Mitchell

Do you ever wonder about the personal lives of those who
serve you: the taxi-driver, the traffic policeman, your barber, your
English teacher—the consultant at the travel bureau?

All day she sits behind a bright brass rail
   Planning proud journeyings in terms that bring
   Far places near; high-colored words that sing,
"The Taj Mahal at Agra," "Kashmir's Vale,"
Spanning wide spaces with her clear detail,   5
   "Sevilla or Fiesole in spring,
   Through the fiords in June." Her words take wing.
She is the minstrel of the great out-trail.

At half-past five she puts her maps away,
   Pins on a gray, meek hat, and braves the sleet,   10
A timid eye on traffic. Dully gray
   The house that harbors her in a gray street,
   The close, sequestered, colorless retreat
Where she was born, where she will always stay.

What does it mean to say that this poem is somewhat cynical?

What other vocations do you know in which the worker's job may be quite out-of-keeping with the life he leads?

In what form is this poem presented? (Check the number of lines, the meter, the rime scheme.)

EIGHT-CYLINDER MAN

Florence Ripley Mastin

In this poem the poet is critical of the person who prizes speed for the mere sake of speed, miles for just sheer miles. Such an individual lives in a kind of abstract world of space and speed. He has no place for the "small life," the little natural beauties about him. It is as if there is no landscape and no summer, the beauty of which he does not recognize when he sees it.

> He grinds the clover at its root
> with a creaking and enormous foot.
> In his circumference vast and dim
> no small life has a place for him.
> The needlepoint of curious moss   5
> where delicate footprints cross,
> the brook composing mountain blues,
> the bereaved and cynical yews,
> columbines dancing on a wall—
> these he has never seen at all.   10
>
> Speed is the only register
> within his mind, and in that blur
> of gas and gleaming chromium
> he adds the swiftly mounting sum
> of miles, a purely abstract space,   15
> and passes summer face to face.

What hollowness of the eight-cylinder man's values is conveyed to you through this poem? In your opinion, what phrases are used satirically and ironically?

Compare this poem with W. H. Davies's poem "Leisure" (p. 99). How are the poems alike in theme? To some persons there is poetry in speed itself. Show how the man in this poem is unaware of any such poetry.

SONG

Adelaide Crapsey

Not all triolets are in playful vein.

> I made my shroud but no one knows,
> So shimmering fine it is and fair,
> With stitches set in even rows.
> I made my shroud but no one knows,
> In door-way where the lilac blows   5
> Humming a little wandering air,
> I made my shroud and no one knows,
> So shimmering fine it is and fair.

What is a shroud? Do you think the poet means a literal shroud, or is the "shroud" a symbol of something else? If so, what?

Does your taste run more to the restrictions of such artificial forms as the triolet or to the freedom of "free verse"? What can be said in favor of your preference?

Try to put the meaning of this poem into a heroic couplet, or a limerick, or a sonnet, or a bit of free verse.

EARTH

Oliver Herford

Here's a bit of verse to set you to thinking!

> If this little world to-night
> Suddenly should fall through space
> In a hissing, headlong flight,
> Shrivelling from off its face,
> As it falls into the sun,   5
> In an instant every trace
> Of the little crawling things—
> Ants, philosophers, and lice,
> Cattle, cockroaches, and kings,
> Beggars, millionaires, and mice,   10
> Men and maggots all as one

As it falls into the sun. . . .
Who can say but at the same
Instant from some planet far
A child may watch us and exclaim: 15
"See the pretty shooting star!"

What did you think of Oliver Herford's list of "little crawling
things"? What point was he trying to make? Do you agree with him?
Why, or why not?
Find some examples of alliteration in the poem.
How can this poem make the sight of a shooting star mean more to
you in the future than it has in the past?

THE BOOK-WORMS *
Robert Burns

Few poets in the English language have as keen a sense of
what a lyric poem is as did the famed Scottish poet Robert Burns.
He even made a brief and ridiculous poem sound important.

Through and through th'inspired leaves,
Ye maggots, make your windings;
But O, respect his lordship's taste,
And spare the golden bindings!

SONG

(from Act I, Scene 3 of The Duenna)
Richard Brinsley Sheridan

Though this song is contained within a play, it can be lifted
from context and enjoyed on its own. The subject matter is life with
daughter rather than life with father. The father is a widower through
whose eyes we see the daughter.

If a daughter you have, she's the plague of your life,
No peace shall you know, tho' you've buried your wife,
At twenty she mocks at the duty you taught her,

* Said to have been written on a splendidly bound but worm-eaten
volume of Shakespeare in a nobleman's library.

O, what a plague is an obstinate daughter.
                 Sighing and whining,   5
                 Dying and pining,
O,what a plague is an obstinate daughter.

When scarce in their teens, they have wit to perplex us,
With letters and lovers for ever they vex us,
While each still rejects the fair suitor you've brought her,   10
O, what a plague is an obstinate daughter.
                 Wrangling and jangling,
                 Flouting and pouting,
O, what a plague is an obstinate daughter.

In the light of your own observations, what truth does the song contain?

Show how the stanzaic pattern is well adapted to the thought and feeling conveyed. Find examples of internal riming. What does this add to the total effect of the lyric?

A DUTCH PROVERB

Matthew Prior

This is a very light-hearted poem, probably written with the tongue in the cheek. It is simply intended to amuse you.

Fire, Water, Woman are Man's Ruin;
Says wise Professor Vander Bruin.
By Flames a House I hir'd was lost
Last year: and I must pay the Cost.
This Spring the Rains o'erflowed my Ground: 5
And my best Flanders Mare was drown'd.
A Slave I am to Clara's Eyes:
The Gipsey knows her Pow'r, and flies.
Fire, Water, Woman are My Ruin:
And great Thy Wisdom, Vander Bruin.   10

How does the poem prove the opening statement? How seriously is the reader to interpret ruin?

What other proverbs do you know? Which ones are stated in verse form? Try rewriting some of the well-known proverbs in verse.

Epitaphs for Three Prominent Persons

Phyllis McGinley

THE INDEPENDENT

So open was his mind, so wide
To welcome winds from every side
That public weather took dominion,
Sweeping him bare of all opinion.

THE STATESMAN

He did not fear his enemies
    Nor their despiteful ends,
But not the seraphs on their knees
    Could save him from his friends.

THE DEMAGOGUE

That trumpet tongue which taught a nation
Loud lessons in vituperation
Teaches it yet another, viz.:
How sweet the noise of silence is.

EPITAPH ON A DENTIST
Anonymous

Stranger, approach this spot with gravity;
John Brown is filling his last cavity.

ON LESLIE MOORE

Anonymous

Here lies what's left
Of Leslie Moore
No Les
No more.

prudence

Don Marquis

Archy is a cockroach who every night types out a poem. Of course, he cannot type capitals and most punctuation, but he can, and does, give us amusing stories and advice.

i do not think a prudent one
will ever aim too high
a cockroach seldom whips a dog
and seldom should he try

and should a locust take a vow   5
to eat a pyramid
he likely would wear out his teeth
before he ever did

i do not think the prudent one
hastes to initiate   10
a sequence of events which he
lacks power to terminate

for should i kick the woolworth tower
so hard i laid it low
it probably might injure me   15
if it fell on my toe

i do not think the prudent one
will be inclined to boast
lest circumstances unforeseen
should get him goat and ghost   20

for should i tell my friends i d drink
the hudson river dry
a tidal wave might come and turn
my statements to a lie

                    archy

What other ways than boasting are suggested as imprudent? What
is your opinion of prudence as a virtue?

Read more of Archy's verses in *Archy and Mehitabel* or *Lives and
Times of Archy and Mehitabel.*

I SOMETIMES THINK

R. P. Lister

This little bit of gentle irony finds a ready response from
most of us.

I sometimes think I shall study to be a lama,
  I shall live by the difficult principles of Zen,
And devote my leisure moments to Japanese drama,
  But I don't know when.

I sometimes think I shall lock myself in an attic   5
  And live on bread and water discreetly mixed,
Till life grows clear and my thoughts are pure and ecstatic,
  But the time's not fixed.

I sometimes think I shall go to the wide white beaches
  And lie in the sun till I cease to snuffle and cough;   10
There I shall learn what the palm tree says and the wild wave
    teaches.
    But I put it off.

I sometimes think I shall learn to play the sackbut,
  Or do research on the crystal structure of zinc.
In fact, I do very little but lie on my back, but
  I sometimes think.   15

What adjectives would you use to describe Mr. Lister's ambitions?
What do you "sometimes think" you will sometime do?

INSCRIPTION FOR THE CEILING OF A BEDROOM
Dorothy Parker

Here's another bit of playful cynicism by one of our most witty versifiers.

Daily dawns another day;
I must up, to make my way.
Though I dress and drink and eat,
Move my fingers and my feet,
Learn a little, here and there,   5
Weep and laugh and sweat and swear,
Hear a song, or watch a stage,
Leave some words upon a page,
Claim a foe, or hail a friend—
Bed awaits me at the end.   10

Though I go in pride and strength,
I'll come back to bed at length.
Though I walk in blinded woe,
Back to bed I'm bound to go.
High my heart, or bowed my head,   15
All my days but lead to bed.
Up, and out, and on; and then
Ever back to bed again,
Summer, Winter, Spring, and Fall—
I'm a fool to rise at all!   20

What do you think of the title?
For a collection of Dorothy Parker's poems see page 11.

BUSINESS
Arthur Guiterman

Arthur Guiterman is another of America's most popular writers of humorous poetry.

Merchants have their ups and downs
Whether selling shoes or gowns;

Doctors find collections slow,
Dentists often have to owe,
Lawyers feel the need of cash, 5
Even bankers go to smash,
Railroads have to beg for gold,
Luggage dealers seem to hold
One eternal bankrupt sale.
Undertakers never fail. 10

DON'T SHAKE THE BOTTLE, SHAKE YOUR MOTHER-IN-LAW
Phyllis McGinley

The title of this poem is, of course, fair warning not to take
it seriously. It is a gay bit of satire directed at the idea that all our
ills ("angina, arthritis, abdominal pains") are psychosomatic, a big
word which means caused by mental or emotional disturbance.

When I was young and full of rhymes
   And all my days were salady,
Almost I could enjoy the times
   I caught some current malady.
Then, cheerful, knocked upon my door 5
   The jocular physician,
With tonics and with comfort for
   My innocent condition.
Then friends would fetch me flowers
   And nurses rub my back, 10
And I could talk for hours
   Concerning my attack.
But now, when vapors dog me,
   What solace do I find?
My cronies can't endure me. 15
The doctors scorn to cure me,
And, though I ail, assure me
   It's all a state of mind.

It's psychosomatic, now, psychosomatic.
Whatever you suffer is psychosomatic. 20

Your liver's a-quiver? You're feeling infirm?
Dispose of the notion you harbor a germ.
Angina,
　Arthritis,
　　Abdominal pain—   25
They're nothing but symptoms of marital strain.
They're nothing but proof that your love life is minus.
The ego is aching
Instead of the sinus.
So face up and brace up and stifle that sneeze.   30
It's psychosomatic. And ten dollars, please.

　　There was a time that I recall,
　　　If one grew pale or thinnish,
　　The pundits loved to lay it all
　　　On foods unvitaminish,   35
　　Or else, dogmatic, would maintain
　　　Infection somewhere acted.
　　And when they'd shorn the tonsils twain,
　　　They pulled the tooth impacted.
　　But now that orgies dental   40
　　　Have made a modish halt,
　　Your ills today are mental
　　　And likely all your fault.
　　Now specialists inform you,
　　　While knitting of their brows,   45
　　Your pain, though sharp and shooting,
　　Is caused, beyond disputing,
　　Because you hate commuting
　　　Or can't abide your spouse.

It's psychosomatic, now, psychosomatic.   50
You fell down the stairway? It's psychosomatic.
That sprain of the ankle while waxing the floors—
You did it on purpose to get out of chores.
Nephritis,
　Neuritis,   55
　　A case of the ague?
You're just giving in to frustrations that plague you.

201

You long to be coddled, beloved, acclaimed,
So you caught the sniffles.
And aren't you ashamed! 60
And maybe they're right. But I sob through my wheezes,
"They've taken the fun out of having diseases."

Read the poem aloud and show that the rhythm and rimes contribute to the light touch with which Miss McGinley treats her subject.

How do the last two lines prove conclusively that the poem is to be taken tongue-in-cheek?

WHAT MR. ROBINSON THINKS

James Russell Lowell

During the Mexican War (1846–48) James Russell Lowell, under the pseudonym of Hosea Biglow, wrote some poems (called the *Biglow Papers*) denouncing that war. These poems, written in the dialect of a New England farmer of that era, have lived on in our literary tradition, because they express so amusingly one side of the eternal conflict between those who believe in "my country, right or wrong" and those who believe that if some policy of our country is wrong—even a war—it should be opposed.

Lowell believed the Mexican War was an unrighteous war, and opposed it through the satire of the *Biglow Papers*.

Guvener B. is a sensible man;
He stays to his home an' looks arter his folks;
He draws his furrer ez straight ez he can,
An' into nobody's tater-patch pokes;—
        But John P. 5
        Robinson he
Sez he wunt vote fer Guvener B.

My! aint it terrible? What shall we du?
We can't never chose him o' course,—thet's flat;
Guess we shall hev to come round, (Don't you?) 10
An' go in fer thunder an' guns, an' all that;
        Fer John P.
        Robinson he
Sez he wunt vote fer Guvener B.

Gineral C. is a dreffle smart man: 15
  He's ben on all sides thet give places or pelf,
But consistency still wuz a part of his plan,—
  He's ben true to *one* party,—an' thet is himself;
        So John P.
        Robinson he   20
      Sez he shall vote fer Gineral C.

Gineral C. he goes in fer the war;
  He don't vally principle more'n an old cud;
Wut did God make us raytional creeturs fer,
  But glory an' gunpowder, plunder an' blood?   25
        So John P.
        Robinson he
      Sez he shall vote fer Gineral C.

We were gittin' on nicely up here to our village,
  With good old idees o' wut's right an' wut aint,   30
We kind o' thought Christ went again' war an' pillage,
  An' thet eppyletts worn't the best mark of a saint;
        But John P.
        Robinson he
      Sez this kind o' thing's an exploded idee.   35

The side of our country must ollers be took,
  An' President Polk, you know, *he* is our country;
An' the angel thet writes all our sins in a book
  Puts the *debit* to him, an' to us the *per contry;*
        An' John P.   40
        Robinson he
      Sez this is his view o' the thing to a T.

Parson Wilbur he calls all these argiments lies;
  Sez they're nothin' on airth but jest *fee, faw, fum:*—
An' thet all this big talk of our destinies   45
  Is half ov it ign'ance, an' t'other half rum;
        But John P.
        Robinson he
      Sez it aint no sech thing; an', of course, so must we.

Parson Wilbur sez *he* never heerd in his life   50
    Thet th' Apostles rigged out in their swaller-tail coats
An' marched round in front of a drum an' a fife,
    To git some on 'em office, an' some on 'em votes;
        But John P.
        Robinson he   55
    Sez they didn't know everythin' down in Judee.

Wal, it's a marcy we've gut folks to tell us
    The rights an' the wrongs o' these matters, I vow,
God sends country lawyers, an' other wise fellers,
    To drive the world's team wen it gits in a slough;   60
        Fer John P.
        Robinson he
    Sez the world'll go right, ef he hollers out Gee!

Be sure you can translate all the dialect into understandable English. What are the meanings of: "into nobody's tater-patch pokes," "an old cud," "eppyletts worn't the best mark of a saint," "the *debit* to him, an' to us the *per contry*," "ef he hollers out Gee!"? How does the use of dialect add to the effect of the poem? Detract from it?

What, if anything, in the poem do you disagree with?

MEN

Dorothy Parker

They hail you as their morning star
Because you are the way you are.
If you return the sentiment,
They'll try to make you different;
And once they have you, safe and sound,   5
They want to change you all around.
Your moods and ways they put a curse on;
They'd make of you another person.
They cannot let you go your gait;
They influence and educate.   10
They'd alter all that they admired.
They make me sick, they make me tired.

SONG OF THE CHATTAHOOCHEE

Sidney Lanier

Few poets have been more successful at creating music in words than Sidney Lanier.

In "Song of the Chattahoochee" practically every musical device known to poets has been made use of. Almost magically the poet recreates the rippling stream moving downward to the ocean in answer to the call of Duty.

Read the poem first to get the meaning and then read it aloud to hear the exquisite music.

Out of the hills of Habersham,
Down the valleys of Hall,
I hurry amain to reach the plain,
Run the rapid and leap the fall,
Split at the rock and together again,   5
Accept my bed, or narrow or wide,
And flee from folly on every side
With a lover's pain to attain the plain
     Far from the hills of Habersham,
     Far from the valleys of Hall.   10

All down the hills of Habersham,
All through the valleys of Hall,
The rushes cried, *Abide, abide,*
The willful waterweeds held me thrall,
The laving laurel turned my tide,   15
The ferns and the fondling grass said *Stay,*
The dewberry dipped for to work delay,
And the little reeds sighed, *Abide, abide,*
     Here in the hills of Habersham,
     Here in the valleys of Hall.   20

High o'er the hills of Habersham,
Veiling the valleys of Hall,
The hickory told me manifold
Fair tales of shade, the poplar tall
Wrought me her shadowy self to hold,   25

The chestnut, the oak, the walnut, the pine,
Overleaning, with flickering meaning and sign,
Said, *Pass not, so cold, these manifold*
　　Deep shades of the hills of Habersham,
　　These glades in the valleys of Hall.　　　　　　30

　And oft in the hills of Habersham,
　　And oft in the valleys of Hall,
The white quartz shone, and the smooth brook-stone
Did bar me of passage with friendly brawl,
And many a luminous jewel lone　　　　　　　　35
—Crystals clear or a-cloud with mist,
Ruby, garnet, and amethyst—
Made lures with the lights of streaming stone
　　In the clefts of the hills of Habersham,
　　In the beds of the valleys of Hall.　　　　　　40

　But oh, not the hills of Habersham,
　　And oh, not the valleys of Hall
Avail: I am fain for to water the plain.
Downward the voices of Duty call—
Downward, to toil and be mixed with the main;　　45
The dry fields burn, and the mills are to turn,
And a myriad flowers mortally yearn,
And the lordly main from beyond the plain
　　Calls o'er the hills of Habersham,
　　Calls through the valleys of Hall.　　　　　　50

Note the use of *or–or* for *either–or* in line 6. What does *fain* in line 43 mean?

Point out examples of the various musical devices used: rhythm, rime, alliteration, refrain.

What great lesson is taught by this poem?

RUBÁIYÁT OF OMAR KHAYYÁM
Edward FitzGerald

　　The Rubáiyát (quatrains) of the Persian poet Omar Khayyám (Omar, the Tent Maker), was put into delightful English verse by Edward FitzGerald. Omar's praise of "wine, woman, and song" is pagan and worldly, and a bit wicked. Perhaps that is why it is so popular! The advice to "eat, drink, and be merry" has always been tempting.

A few of the best known quatrains are printed here.

VII

Come, fill the Cup, and in the fire of Spring
Your Winter garment of Repentance fling:
  The Bird of Time has but a little way
To flutter—and the Bird is on the Wing.

VIII

Whether at Naishapur or Babylon,   5
Whether the Cup with sweet or bitter run,
  The wine of Life keeps oozing drop by drop,
The Leaves of Life keep falling one by one.

XII

A Book of Verses underneath the Bough,
A Jug of Wine, a Loaf of Bread—and Thou   10
  Beside me singing in the Wilderness—
Oh, Wilderness were Paradise enow!

XIII

Some for the Glories of This World; and some
Sigh for the Prophet's Paradise to come;
  Ah, take the Cash, and let the Credit go,   15
Nor heed the rumble of a distant Drum!

XVI

The Worldly Hope men set their Hearts upon
Turns Ashes—or it prospers; and anon,
  Like Snow upon the Desert's dusty Face,
Lighting a little hour or two—is gone.   20

XXI

Ah, my Belovèd, fill the Cup that clears
Today of past Regrets and future Fears:
  Tomorrow!—Why, Tomorrow I may be
Myself with Yesterday's Sev'n thousand Years.

XXIV

Ah, make the most of what we yet may spend,   25
Before we too into the Dust descend;
   Dust into Dust, and under Dust to lie,
Sans Wine, sans Song, sans Singer, and—sans End!

LXXI

The Moving Finger writes; and, having writ,
Moves on: nor all your Piety nor Wit   30
   Shall lure it back to cancel half a Line,
Nor all your Tears wash out a Word of it.

LXXIV

Yesterday *This* Day's Madness did prepare;
Tomorrow's Silence, Triumph, or Despair:
   Drink! for you know not whence you came, nor why: 35
Drink! for you know not why you go, nor where.

XCVI

Yet Ah, that Spring should vanish with the Rose!
That Youth's sweet-scented manuscript should close!
   The Nightingale that in the branches sang,
Ah whence, and whither flown again, who knows?   40

XCIX

Ah Love! could you and I with Him conspire
To grasp this sorry Scheme of Things entire,
   Would not we shatter it to bits—and then
Re-mould it nearer to the Heart's Desire!

Which of these quatrains had you ever heard before? Which ones do you like? What do you think of their pagan attitude toward pleasure?

DANIEL AT BREAKFAST
Phyllis McGinley

His paper propped against the electric toaster
   (Nicely adjusted to his morning use),

Daniel at breakfast studies world disaster
And sips his orange juice.

The words dismay him. Headlines shrilly chatter   5
Of famine, storm, death, pestilence, decay.
Daniel is gloomy, reaching for the butter.
He shudders at the way

War stalks the planet still, and men know hunger,
Go shelterless, betrayed, may perish soon.   10
The coffee's weak again. In sudden anger
Daniel throws down his spoon

And broods a moment on the kitchen faucet
The plumber mended, but has mended ill;
Recalls tomorrow means a dental visit,   15
Laments the grocery bill.

Then, having shifted from his human shoulder
The universal woe, he drains his cup,
Rebukes the weather (surely turning colder),
Crumples his napkin up   20
And, kissing his wife abruptly at the door,
Stamps fiercely off to catch the 8:04.

INVESTOR'S SOLILOQUY
Kenneth Ward

This is a parody of the famous soliloquy "To be or not to be,"
in Shakespeare's *Hamlet*. To enjoy it you need to be familiar with
both the original and the language of the stock market.

To buy, or not to buy; that is the question:
Whether 'tis nobler in the mind to suffer
The slings and arrows of an outrageous market,
Or to take cash against a sea of troubles,
And by selling, end them. To buy, to keep—   5
No more; and by this keeping, to say we end
The bear trend and the thousand natural shocks
That stocks are heir to—'tis a consummation

Devoutly to be wish'd—To buy, to keep—
To keep? Perchance on margin! Ay, there's the rub!   10
For in that margining what dreams may come,
When we have shuffled off our buying power,
Must give us pause. There's the respect
That makes calamity of so long a position.
For who would bear the whips and scorns of debit balances,   15
The broker's interest, the shorts' contumely,
The pangs of dispriz'd appreciation, the market's delay,
The insolence of bankers, and the spurns
That patient merit of the unworthy takes,
When he himself might the quietus make   20
With a bare short sale? Who would losses bear
To grunt and sweat under a falling market,
But that the dread of something after selling,
The undiscover'd rally—from whose bourn
No short seller returns, puzzles the will   25
And makes us rather bear those losses we have
Than fly to others that we know not of?
Thus ambivalence does make cowards of us all.
And thus the native hue of resolution
Is sicklied o'er with the pale cast of doubt   30
And enterprises of great pith and moment,
With this regard, their currents turn awry,
And lose the name of profits.

Perhaps your teacher will ask one member of the class to read the soliloquy in *Hamlet* and another to explain the brokerage terms. Then you can read the parody again, and this time it will, I hope, seem funny to you. It is, I assure you, a quite clever parody.

SESTINA OF YOUTH AND AGE

Gelett Burgess

When quite young, a boy rarely realizes that in the son the father may be reliving his youthful hopes, wild desires, and driving ambition. Later perhaps the boy understands.

Mr. Burgess has expressed this development of understanding in one of the most difficult of the French verse forms, the sestina. First read the poem for the thought; then study the complex form.

My father died when I was all too young,	1
And he too old, too crowded with his care,	2
For me to know he knew my hot fierce hopes;	3
Youth sees wide chasms between itself and Age—	4
How could I think he, too, had lived my life?	5 5
My dreams were all of war, and his of rest.	6
And so he sleeps (please God), at last at rest,	6
And, it may be, with soul refreshed, more young	1
Than when he left me, for that other life—	5
Free, for a while, at least, from that old Care,	2 10
The hard, relentless torturer of his age,	4
That cooled his youth, and bridled all his hopes.	3
For now I know he had the longing hopes,	3
The wild desires of youth, and all the rest	6
Of my ambitions ere he came to age;	4 15
He, too, was bold, when he was free and young—	1
Had I but known that he could feel, and care!	2
How could I know the secret of his life?	5
In my own youth I see his early life	5
So reckless, and so full of flaming hopes—	3 20
I see him jubilant, without a care,	2
The days too short, and grudging time for rest;	6
He knew the wild delight of being young—	1
Shall I, too, know the calmer joys of age?	4
His words come back, to mind me of that age	4 25
When, lovingly, he watched my broadening life—	5
And, dreaming of the days when he was young,	1
Smiled at my joys, and shared my fears and hopes.	3
His words still live, for in my heart they rest,	6
Too few not to be kept with jealous care!	2 30
Ah, little did I know how he could care!	2
That, in my youth, lay joys to comfort age!	4

Not in this world, for him, was granted rest,   6
But as he lived, in me, a happier life,   5
He prayed more earnestly to win my hopes   3   35
Than ever for his own, when he was young!   1

Envoy

He once was young; I too must fight with Care;   1,2
He knew my hopes, and I must share his age;   3,4
God grant my life be worthy, too, of rest!   5,6   40

The sestina consists of six six-line stanzas and a three-line envoy (or postscript). The stanzas do not rime, but the six end-words are the same in all the stanzas and are arranged in this strict sequence:

```
stanza 1—1  2  3  4  5  6
stanza 2—6  1  5  2  4  3
stanza 3—3  6  4  1  2  5
stanza 4—5  3  2  6  1  4
stanza 5—4  5  1  3  6  2
stanza 6—2  4  6  5  3  1
```

(A little study will reveal to you the system providing the sequence.)

All six words are used in the envoy, half of them within the lines and the other half at the ends. The usual order is: line 1—2,5; line 2—4,3; line 3—6,1. Mr. Burgess has allowed himself a little variation in the envoy: line 1—1,2; line 2—3,4; line 3—5,6.

The complexity of this highly artificial form makes it more of a metrical exercise than anything else; but whether or not you enjoy the skill with which this poet triumphs over the limitations of this difficult form, enjoy his impressive portrayal of the growing understanding of a father by a son.

OZYMANDIAS

Percy Bysshe Shelley

Shelley, considered by his contemporaries to be a rebel, is concerned in this sonnet with the ancient theme of the fleetingness of life and the frailty of human power. Even a great Egyptian king, builder of many palaces and temples decorated with sculptures of himself done by sculptors as a command performance—even this glory passes.

I met a traveler from an antique land
Who said: "Two vast and trunkless legs of stone

Stand in the desert . . . Near them, on the sand,
Half sunk, a shattered visage lies, whose frown,
And wrinkled lip, and sneer of cold command,   5
Tell that its sculptor well those passions read
Which yet survive, stamped on these lifeless things,
The hand that mocked them, and the heart that fed;
And on the pedestal these words appear;
'My name is Ozymandias, king of kings;   10
Look on my works, ye Mighty, and despair!'
Nothing beside remains. Round the decay
Of that colossal wreck, boundless and bare
The lone and level sands stretch far away."

With what human emotion were you involved as you read?
What evidently did Ozymandias himself not see in the sculptor's
creation? Or what might have been the risk the artist took?
What irony is contained in the words on the pedestal?

ON THE GRASSHOPPER AND CRICKET
John Keats

A grasshopper and a cricket are not exactly foreign to you.
Suppose that on a certain occasion, inspired by the sound the cricket
makes, you and a friend decided then and there to compete with one
another in writing a sonnet, the subject matter being concerned with
a grasshopper and a cricket. You might even time yourselves, or a
third party could time you both. Under such circumstances this sonnet
was written—in fun and in competition.

The poetry of earth is never dead:
    When all the birds are faint with the hot sun,
    And hide in cooling trees, a voice will run
From hedge to hedge about the new-mown mead;
That is the grasshopper's—he takes the lead   5
    In summer luxury,—he has never done
    With his delights, for when tired out with fun
He rests at ease beneath some pleasant weed.

The poetry of earth is ceasing never:
   On a lone winter evening, when the frost   10
Has wrought a silence, from the stove there shrills
The cricket's song, in warmth increasing ever,
   And seems to one, in drowsiness half-lost,
The grasshopper's among some grassy hills.

What is "the poetry of earth"? Why is it "never dead"? What is implied about the world of nature in the last line?

WHEN I HAVE FEARS

John Keats

It is easy to forget that young people, as well as old, experienced ones, have their sometimes well-founded fears. Tuberculosis afflicted the Keats family. The dread of that disease, in 1817, seems to have weighed heavily upon this young man of twenty-two. There was so much writing and reading and adventuring he wanted to do! But the old fear was there: he might not get to accomplish these riches. This young man's literary fame rests upon what he accomplished between the ages of twenty-two and twenty-five. He was dead at twenty-five.

When I have fears that I may cease to be
Before my pen has gleaned my teeming brain,
Before high-piled books, in charactery,
Hold like rich garners the full ripened grain;
When I behold, upon the night's starred face,   5
Huge cloudy symbols of a high romance,
And think that I may never live to trace
Their shadows, with the magic hand of chance;
And when I feel, fair creature of an hour,
That I shall never look upon thee more,   10
Never have relish in the faery power
Of unreflecting love—then on the shore
Of the wide world I stand alone, and think
Till love and fame to nothingness do sink.

What is your emotional response to this poem? What emotion is Keats expressing? What do you make of the last line?

LET ME NOT TO THE MARRIAGE OF TRUE MINDS
William Shakespeare

Shakespeare, the greatest of all English poets, gives us a sonnet on the unchanging permanence of true love. "Love's not Time's fool," he says; "it is an ever-fixed mark" that "bears it out even to the edge of doom."

Let me not to the marriage of true minds
Admit impediments. Love is not love
Which alters when it alteration finds,
Or bends with the remover to remove:
O, no! it is an ever-fixed mark,   5
That looks on tempests and is never shaken;
It is the star to every wandering bark,
Whose worth's unknown, although his height be taken.
Love's not Time's fool, though rosy lips and cheeks
Within his bending sickle's compass come;   10
Love alters not with his brief hours and weeks,
But bears it out even to the edge of doom.
    If this be error, and upon me prov'd,
    I never writ, nor no man ever lov'd.

Why did Shakespeare speak of "the marriage of true *minds*"? What do you think he means by "love" in this sonnet?

What word is modified by the clauses in lines 3 and 4? What do these lines mean?

Explain the metaphor in lines 7 and 8.

Write out in your own words the meaning of this sonnet, idea by idea.

DOVER BEACH
Matthew Arnold

This wonderful lyric was written in the nineteenth century, but no later poet has better expressed the present confused state of the world than Matthew Arnold did in the last stanza of this poem.

The first two stanzas indicate how the sea brings to mind the sadness of human misery. Then comes the magnificent third stanza, which surely you will not be able to read unmoved.

The sea is calm to-night.
The tide is full, the moon lies fair
Upon the straits:—on the French coast the light
Gleams and is gone; the cliffs of England stand,
Glimmering and vast, out in the tranquil bay.   5
Come to the window, sweet is the night air!
Only, from the long line of spray
Where the sea meets the moon-blanched land,
Listen! you hear the grating roar
Of pebbles which the waves draw back, and fling,   10
At their return, up the high strand,
Begin, and cease, and then again begin,
With tremulous cadence slow, and bring
The eternal note of sadness in.

Sophocles long ago   15
Heard it on the Ægæan, and it brought
Into his mind the turbid ebb and flow
Of human misery; we
Find also in the sound a thought,
Hearing it by this distant northern sea.   20
The Sea of Faith
Was once, too, at the full, and round earth's shore
Lay like the folds of a bright girdle furled.
But now I only hear
Its melancholy, long, withdrawing roar,   25
Retreating, to the breath
Of the night wind, down the vast edges drear
And naked shingles of the world.

Ah, love, let us be true
To one another! for the world, which seems   30
To lie before us like a land of dreams,
So various, so beautiful, so new,
Hath really neither joy, nor love, nor light,

Nor certitude, nor peace, nor help for pain;
And we are here as on a darkling plain   35
Swept with confused alarms of struggle and flight
Where ignorant armies clash by night.

To get the full impact of the beautiful imagery at the beginning
of the poem you must be sure to reconstruct the images in your own
mind.

What events have caused "The Sea of Faith" to retreat? What ad-
vice does Matthew Arnold give to make life endurable?

TO A WATERFOWL

William Cullen Bryant

John Bigelow, Bryant's biographer, describes the situation
which inspired this poem as follows: "The sun had already set, leaving
behind it one of those brilliant seas of chrysolite and opal which often
flood the New England skies, and while pausing to contemplate the
rosy splendor with rapt adoration, a solitary bird made its winged way
along the illuminated horizon. He watched the lone wanderer until
it was lost in the distance. He then went on with new strength and
courage. When he reached the house where he was to stop for the
night, he immediately sat down and wrote the lines 'To a Water-
fowl,' the concluding verse of which will perpetuate to future ages
the lesson on faith which the scene had impressed upon him."

Whither, midst falling dew,
While glow the heavens with the last steps of day,
Far, through their rosy depths, dost thou pursue
Thy solitary way?

Vainly the fowler's eye   5
Might mark thy distant flight to do thee wrong,
As, darkly seen against the crimson sky,
Thy figure floats along.

Seek'st thou the plashy brink
Of weedy lake, or marge of river wide,   10
Or where the rocking billows rise and sink
On the chafed ocean-side?

217

There is a Power whose care
Teaches thy way along that pathless coast—
The desert and illimitable air—   15
    Lone wandering, but not lost.

All day thy wings have fanned,
At that far height, the cold, thin atmosphere,
Yet stoop not, weary, to the welcome land,
    Though the dark night is near.   20

And soon that toil shall end;
Soon shalt thou find a summer home, and rest,
And scream among thy fellows; reeds shall bend,
    Soon, o'er thy sheltered nest.

Thou'rt gone, the abyss of heaven   25
Hath swallowed up thy form; yet, on my heart
Deeply has sunk the lesson thou hast given,
    And shall not soon depart:

He who, from zone to zone,
Guides through the boundless sky thy certain flight, 30
In the long way that I must tread alone,
    Will lead my steps aright.

What is the lesson Bryant learned from the bird? (You might be
wise to commit the last stanza to memory.)
    Explain the meter of the unusual stanza Bryant used. Did you find
it pleasing or unpleasant to the ear?
    The theme or underlying meaning of the poem is stated twice.
Quote the two statements of theme. How much would the poem suffer
if the last stanza were omitted?

ICHABOD

John Greenleaf Whittier

    This poem is a dirge. As such it does not lament the death
of a person but the action of a living being. That being was the famous
Daniel Webster whose speech in 1850 in Whittier's opinion showed
a too compromising spirit on the issue of slavery. Whittier, in this

powerful poem, conveys his feelings about Webster's action. The name
Ichabod means *the glory has departed.*

> So fallen! so lost! the light withdrawn
>   Which once he wore!
> The glory from his gray hairs gone
>   Forevermore!
>
> Revile him not, the Tempter hath   5
>   A snare for all;
> And pitying tears, not scorn and wrath,
>   Befit his fall!
>
> Oh, dumb be passion's stormy rage,
>   When he who might   10
> Have lighted up and led his age,
>   Falls back in night.
>
> Scorn! would the angels laugh, to mark
>   A bright soul driven,
> Fiend-goaded, down the endless dark,   15
>   From hope and heaven!
>
> Let not the land once proud of him
>   Insult him now,
> Nor brand with deeper shame his dim,
>   Dishonored brow.   20
>
> But let its humbled sons, instead,
>   From sea to lake,
> A long lament, as for the dead,
>   In sadness make.
>
> Of all we loved and honored, naught   25
>   Save power remains;
> A fallen angel's pride of thought,
>   Still strong in chains.
>
> All else is gone; from those great eyes
>   The soul has fled: 30
> When faith is lost, when honor dies,
>   The man is dead.

Then, pay the reverence of old days
   To his dead fame;
Walk backward, with averted gaze,   35
   And hide the shame!

What kind of anger is expressed in this poem? Behind the anger is there fairness of judgment?

What, according to the poem, was the motivation for Webster's action?

In what ways does the stanzaic pattern differ from the ballad stanza or from the common measure?

BIRCHES

Robert Frost

Robert Frost, certainly one of America's greatest poets, likes to describe some simple facet of New England farm life and then philosophize about it. His poems seem disarmingly simple, but they are rich in thought and emotion.

In the following poem he tells about the farm boy's pleasure in "swinging birches."

When I see birches bend to left and right
Across the line of straighter darker trees,
I like to think some boy's been swinging them.
But swinging doesn't bend them down to stay.
Ice storms do that. Often you must have seen them   5
Loaded with ice a sunny winter morning
After a rain. They click upon themselves
As the breeze rises, and turn many-colored
As the stir cracks and crazes their enamel.
Soon the sun's warmth makes them shed crystal shells   10
Shattering and avalanching on the snow crust—
Such heaps of broken glass to sweep away
You'd think the inner dome of heaven had fallen.
They are dragged to the withered bracken by the load,
And they seem not to break; though, once they are bowed   15
So low for long, they never right themselves:
You may see their trunks arching in the woods
Years afterward, trailing their leaves on the ground

Like girls on hands and knees that throw their hair
Before them over their heads to dry in the sun. 20
But I was going to say when Truth broke in
With all her matter of fact about the ice storm
(Now am I free to be poetical?)
I should prefer to have some boy bend them
As he went out and in to fetch the cows— 25
Some boy too far from town to learn baseball,
Whose only play was what he found himself,
Summer or winter, and could play alone.
One by one he subdued his father's trees
By riding them down over and over again 30
Until he took the stiffness out of them,
And not one but hung limp, not one was left
For him to conquer. He learned all there was
To learn about not launching out too soon
And so not carrying the tree away 35
Clear to the ground. He always kept his poise
To the top branches, climbing carefully
With the same pains you use to fill a cup
Up to the brim, and even above the brim.
Then he flung outward, feet first, with a swish, 40
Kicking his way down through the air to the ground.
So was I once myself a swinger of birches;
And so I dream of going back to be.
It's when I'm weary of considerations,
And life is too much like a pathless wood 45
Where your face burns and tickles with the cobwebs
Broken across it, and one eye is weeping
From a twig's having lashed across it open.
I'd like to get away from earth awhile
And then come back to it and begin over. 50
May no fate willfully misunderstand me
And half grant what I wish and snatch me away
Not to return. Earth's the right place for love:
I don't know where it's likely to go better.
I'd like to go by climbing a birch tree, 55
And climb black branches up a snow-white trunk

Toward heaven, till the tree could bear no more,
But dipped its top and set me down again.
That would be good both going and coming back.
One could do worse than be a swinger of birches.   60

What change in the pattern of human life would Frost like to make?
How did the birch trees suggest this idea to him? Do you ever have a
desire for a similar change? If so, what do you do about it?

DEOR'S LAMENT

(from the Old English)

Deor

Deor is a scop or minstrel who has been superseded by an-
other singer. He is, in this early Old English lyric, consoling himself
by recalling others who have met with misfortune. The poem has been
referred to as "the father of all English lyrics."

Deor first calls to mind the legendary smith Weland, who was held
slave by Nithhad and cruelly crippled. The first three stanzas relate
Weland's experiences and his revenge. (Weland killed Nithhad's two
sons, drugged and violated the daughter Beadohild.) The fourth and
fifth stanzas explain themselves. In the last stanza Deor states his con-
clusion (that "God moves in a mysterious way His wonders to per-
form") and tells his own troubles.

The original Old English poem is written in the Anglo-Saxon verse
form described on page 54. Additional interest is found in the refrain.

Weland, the smith, knew woe upon woe,
Exile he knew, and the winter's cold sting,
With companions of hardship, sorrow, despair;
And further ill-fated when held captive by Nithhad,
Who knew him to be the better man,   5
And slit his sinews, thus crippling him.
    That passed over; likewise may this.

Her brothers' death Beadohild bore,
Bore much better than her own plight
When she knew the burden of her womb,   10
Knew for certain a child she'd bear;
Could not think lightly of what must come to pass.
    That passed over; likewise may this.

From many and oft have we heard
Of Beadohild's fate; of her father's boundless love,   15
Which left him grievous and reft of sleep.
   That passed over; likewise may this.

For thirty years Theodric ruled
The stronghold of the Maerings, as many knew.
   That passed over; likewise may this.   20

Of Eormanric's rule we've heard them sing,
He of the wolfish temper. Wide sway he held
In the Gothic realm, this grim king.
Many a warrior, sorrow-bound and woe-expecting,
Wished this rule might come to an end.   25
   That passed over; likewise may this.

The man bereft of joys in sorrow sits;
His mind, in gloom; to him it seems
His measure of misery knows no end.
But think he may how in this wide world   30
The wise Lord works in divers ways,
Granting honor and fame to many a man
And to others a sifting of sorrow.
I have this to say of myself:
Once a minstrel of the Heodenings, I,   35
Deor, my name, dear to my lord.
I had a good job and gracious lord
For many years until Heorrenda,
Full skillful in song, came and took over
My land once graciously granted to me.   40
   That passed over; likewise may this.

THANATOPSIS

William Cullen Bryant

   Thanatopsis means "a looking at death." Most of this poem, which is one of the best-known lyrics in American literature, was written when Bryant was only eighteen years old. In majestic blank

verse, this thoughtful teen-ager records the comfort he receives from
"Nature's teachings" when thoughts of death make him "shudder and
grow sick at heart."

To him who, in the love of Nature, holds
Communion with her visible forms, she speaks
A various language: for his gayer hours
She has a voice of gladness, and a smile
And eloquence of beauty; and she glides   5
Into his darker musings, with a mild
And healing sympathy, that steals away
Their sharpness, ere he is aware. When thoughts
Of the last bitter hour come like a blight
Over thy spirit, and sad images   10
Of the stern agony, and shroud, and pall,
And breathless darkness, and the narrow house,
Make thee to shudder, and grow sick at heart,—
Go forth under the open sky, and list
To Nature's teachings, while from all around—   15
Earth and her waters, and the depths of air—
Comes a still voice:—Yet a few days, and thee
The all-beholding sun shall see no more
In all his course; nor yet in the cold ground,
Where thy pale form was laid, with many tears,   20
Nor in the embrace of ocean, shall exist
Thy image. Earth, that nourished thee, shall claim
Thy growth, to be resolved to earth again;
And, lost each human trace, surrendering up
Thine individual being, shalt thou go   25
To mix forever with the elements;
To be a brother to the insensible rock,
And to the sluggish clod, which the rude swain
Turns with his share, and treads upon. The oak
Shall send his roots abroad, and pierce thy mold. 30
Yet not to thine eternal resting-place
Shalt thou retire alone—nor couldst thou wish
Couch more magnificent. Thou shalt lie down
With patriarchs of the infant world—with kings,

The powerful of the earth—the wise, the good, 35
Fair forms, and hoary seers of ages past,
All in one mighty sepulcher. The hills,
Rock-ribbed, and ancient as the sun; the vales
Stretching in pensive quietness between;
The venerable woods; rivers that move 40
In majesty, and the complaining brooks
That make the meadows green; and, poured round all,
Old Ocean's gray and melancholy waste—
Are but the solemn decorations all
Of the great tomb of man! The golden sun, 45
The planets, all the infinite host of heaven,
Are shining on the sad abodes of death,
Through the still lapse of ages. All that tread
The globe are but a handful to the tribes
That slumber in its bosom. Take the wings 50
Of morning, pierce the Barcan wilderness,
Or lose thyself in the continuous woods
Where rolls the Oregon and hears no sound
Save his own dashings—yet the dead are there;
And millions in those solitudes, since first 55
The flight of years began, have laid them down
In their last sleep—the dead reign there alone!
So shalt thou rest, and what if thou withdraw
In silence from the living; and no friend
Take note of thy departure? All that breathe 60
Will share thy destiny. The gay will laugh
When thou art gone, the solemn brood of care
Plod on, and each one as before will chase
His favorite phantom; yet all these shall leave
Their mirth and their employments, and shall come 65
And make their bed with thee. As the long train
Of ages glides away, the sons of men—
The youth in life's green spring, and he who goes
In the full strength of years, matron and maid,
The speechless babe, and the gray-headed man— 70
Shall one by one be gathered to thy side
By those who in their turn shall follow them.

So live that when thy summons comes to join
The innumerable caravan which moves
To that mysterious realm, where each shall take   75
His chamber in the silent halls of death,
Thou go, not like the quarry-slave at night,
Scourged to his dungeon, but, sustained and soothed
By an unfaltering trust, approach thy grave
Like one who wraps the drapery of his couch   80
About him, and lies down to pleasant dreams.

What does Nature say to Bryant about the certainty of death? What
are the two sources of comfort which Nature offers? What comfort do
you find in these two "teachings" of Nature?

What advice does Bryant offer about preparing for death?

By all means commit to memory the last nine lines. What does "un-
faltering trust" mean to you?

This poem is usually classified as an *ode*. Which characteristics of
an ode does it possess? Which does it lack?

THE GHOSTS OF THE BUFFALOES
Vachel Lindsay

Vachel Lindsay, "the American troubador," specialized in
poetry to be read aloud. In this poem a boy's dream of Indians on
the warpath and of the "fury and foam" of charging buffalo herds is
contrasted with such soft sounds as a cricket's carolling.

This poem *must* be read aloud.

Last night at black midnight I woke with a cry,
The windows were shaking, there was thunder on high,
The floor was a-tremble, the door was a-jar,
White fires, crimson fires, shone from afar.
I rushed to the dooryard. The city was gone.   5
My home was a hut without orchard or lawn.
It was mud-smear and logs near a whispering stream,
Nothing else built by man could I see in my dream . . .

Then . . .
Ghost-kings came headlong, row upon row,   10
Gods of the Indians, torches aglow.

They mounted the bear and the elk and the deer,
And eagles gigantic, aged and sere,
They rode long-horn cattle, they cried "A-la-la."
They lifted the knife, the bow, and the spear,   15
They lifted ghost-torches from dead fires below,
The midnight made grand with the cry "A-la-la."
The midnight made grand with a red-god charge,
A red-god show,
A red-god show,   20
"A-la-la, a-la-la, a-la-la, a-la-la."

With bodies like bronze, and terrible eyes
Came the rank and the file, with catamount cries,
Gibbering, yipping, with hollow-skull clacks,
Riding white bronchos with skeleton backs,   25
Scalp-hunters, beaded and spangled and bad,
Naked and lustful and foaming and mad,
Flashing primeval demoniac scorn,
Blood-thirst and pomp amid darkness reborn,
Power and glory that sleep in the grass   30
While the winds and the snows and the great rains pass.

They crossed the gray river, thousands abreast,
They rode out in infinite lines to the west,
Tide upon tide of strange fury and foam,
Spirits and wraiths, the blue was their home,   35
The sky was their goal where the star-flags are furled,
And on past those far golden splendors they whirled.
They burned to dim meteors, lost in the deep,
And I turned in dazed wonder, thinking of sleep.

And the wind crept by   40
Alone, unkempt, unsatisfied,
The wind cried and cried—
Muttered of massacres long past,
Buffaloes in shambles vast . . .
An owl said: "Hark, what is a-wing?"   45
I heard a cricket carolling,
I heard a cricket carolling,
I heard a cricket carolling.

Then . . .
Snuffing the lightning that crashed from on high   50
Rose royal old buffaloes, row upon row.
The lords of the prairie came galloping by.
And I cried in my heart "A-la-la, a-la-la,
A red-god show,
A red-god show,   55
A-la-la, a-la-la, a-la-la, a-la-la."

Buffaloes, buffaloes, thousands abreast,
A scourge and amazement, they swept to the west.
With black bobbing noses, with red rolling tongues,
Coughing forth steam from their leather-wrapped lungs,   60
Cows with their calves, bulls big and vain,
Goring the laggards, shaking the mane,
Stamping flint feet, flashing moon eyes,
Pompous and owlish, shaggy and wise.

Like sea-cliffs and caves resounded their ranks   65
With shoulders like waves, and undulant flanks.
Tide upon tide of strange fury and foam,
Spirits and wraiths, the blue was their home,
The sky was their goal where the star-flags are furled,
And on past those far golden splendors they whirled.   70
They burned to dim meteors, lost in the deep,
And I turned in dazed wonder, thinking of sleep.

I heard a cricket's cymbals play,
A scarecrow lightly flapped his rags,
And a pan that hung by his shoulder rang,   75
Rattled and thumped in a listless way,
And now the wind in the chimney sang,
The wind in the chimney,
The wind in the chimney,
The wind in the chimney,   80
Seemed to say:—
"Dream, boy, dream,
If you anywise can.
To dream is the work

Of beast or man.   85
Life is the west-going dream-storm's breath,
Life is a dream, the sigh of the skies,
The breath of the stars, that nod on their pillows
With their golden hair mussed over their eyes."

The locust played on his musical wing,   90
Sang to his mate of love's delight.
I heard the whippoorwill's soft fret.
I heard a cricket carolling,
I heard a cricket carolling,
I heard a cricket say: "Good-night, good-night,   95
Good-night, good-night, . . . good-night."

Which of the sight images did you find most vivid? Explain the
imagery in lines 88–89.
Put in your own words what the wind told the boy.
If there is time to do so, this poem can be made into a very effective
exercise in choral reading.

THE BARREL-ORGAN

Alfred Noyes

In this poem you will hear the music from a barrel-organ
being played on a street in London. It is sweet music about spring
and love and nightingales and lilacs; and each listener reacts to it
according to his own age and hopes and experiences.
Join the crowd of listeners and see what the music does for you.

There's a barrel-organ caroling across a golden street
In the City as the sun sinks low;
And the music's not immortal; but the world has made it sweet
And fulfilled it with the sunset glow;
And it pulses through the pleasures of the City and the pain   5
That surround the singing organ like a large eternal light;
And they've given it a glory and a part to play again
In the Symphony that rules the day and night.

2. By the *City* is meant London, especially the older section of London.

And now it's marching onward through the realms of old romance,
   And trolling out a fond familiar tune,   10
And now it's roaring cannon down to fight the King of France,
   And now it's prattling softly to the moon,
And all around the organ there's a sea without a shore
   Of human joys and wonders and regrets;
To remember and to recompense the music evermore   15
   For what the cold machinery forgets. . . .

       Yes; as the music changes,
         Like a prismatic glass,
       It takes the light and ranges
         Through all the moods that pass;   20
       Dissects the common carnival
         Of passions and regrets,
       And gives the world a glimpse of all
         The colors it forgets.

       And there *La Traviata* sighs   25
         Another sadder song;
       And there *Il Trovatore* cries
         A tale of deeper wrong;
       And bolder knights to battle go
         With sword and shield and lance,   30
       Than ever here on earth below
         Have whirled into—a dance!—

Go down to Kew in lilac-time, in lilac-time, in lilac-time;
   Go down to Kew in lilac-time (it isn't far from London!)
And you shall wander hand in hand with love in summer's won-
      derland;   35
   Go down to Kew in lilac-time (it isn't far from London!)

The cherry-trees are seas of bloom and soft perfume and sweet
   perfume,

25. *La Traviata* and *Il Trovatore* are well-known operas by Verdi. In
La Traviata the heroine sings a sad song shortly before her death. In *Il
Trovatore* the troubadour has many misfortunes and is finally executed, un-
knowingly, by his own brother.
33. *Kew:* the Kew Gardens, five or so miles out of London.

The cherry-trees are seas of bloom (and oh, so near to London!)
And there they say, when dawn is high and all the world's a blaze
    of sky
The cuckoo, though he's very shy, will sing a song for Lon-
    don.   40

The nightingale is rather rare and yet they say you'll hear him
    there
At Kew, at Kew in lilac-time (and oh, so near to London!)
The linnet and the throstle, too, and after dark the long halloo
And golden-eyed *tu-whit, tu-whoo* of owls that ogle London.

For Noah hardly knew a bird of any kind that isn't heard   45
At Kew, at Kew in lilac-time (and oh, so near to London!)
And when the rose begins to pout and all the chestnut spires are
    out
You'll hear the rest without a doubt, all chorusing for Lon-
    don:—

Come down to Kew in lilac-time, in lilac-time, in lilac-time;
    Come down to Kew in lilac-time (it isn't far from London!)   50
*And you shall wander hand in hand with love in summer's won-
    derland,*
    Come down to Kew in lilac-time (it isn't far from London!)

And then the troubadour begins to thrill the golden street,
    In the City as the sun sinks low;
And in all the gaudy busses there are scores of weary feet   55
Marking time, sweet time, with a dull mechanic beat,
And a thousand hearts are plunging to a love they'll never meet,
Through the meadows of the sunset, through the poppies and the
    wheat,
    In the land where the dead dreams go.

Verdi, Verdi, when you wrote *Il Trovatore* did you dream   60
    Of the City when the sun sinks low,
Of the organ and the monkey and the many-coloured stream
On the Piccadilly pavement, of the myriad eyes that seem
To be litten for a moment with a wild Italian gleam

As *A che la morte* parodies the world's eternal theme   65
    And pulses with the sunset-glow?

There's a thief, perhaps, that listens with a face of frozen stone
    In the City as the sun sinks low;
There's a portly man of business with a balance of his own,
There's a clerk and there's a butcher of a soft reposeful tone,   70
And they're all of them returning to the heavens they have known:
They are crammed and jammed in busses and—they're each of
        them alone
    In the land where the dead dreams go. . . .

There's a labourer that listens to the voices of the dead
    In the City as the sun sinks low;   75
And his hand begins to tremble and his face is rather red
As he sees a loafer watching him and—there he turns his head
And stares into the sunset where his April love is fled,
For he hears her softly singing and his lonely soul is led
    Through the land where the dead dreams go.   80

There's an old and haggard demi-rep, it's ringing in her ears,
    In the City as the sun sinks low;
With the wild and empty sorrow of the love that blights and sears,
Oh, and if she hurries onward, then be sure, be sure she hears,
Hears and bears the bitter burden of the unforgotten years,   85
And her laugh's a little harsher and her eyes are brimmed with
        tears
    For the land where the dead dreams go.

There's a barrel-organ caroling across a golden street
    In the City as the sun sinks low;
Though the music's only Verdi there's a world to make it sweet   90
Just as yonder yellow sunset where the earth and heaven meet
Mellows all the sooty City! Hark, a hundred thousand feet
Are marching on to glory through the poppies and the wheat
    In the land where the dead dreams go.

65. *A che la morte* (Ah that death): an aria sung by the troubadour from
his prison window.

So, it's Jeremiah, Jeremiah,   95
    What have you to say
When you meet the garland girls
    Tripping on their way?
All around my gala hat
    I wear a wreath of roses   100
(A long and lonely year it is
    I've waited for the May!)
If any one should ask you,
    The reason why I wear it is—
My own love, my true love   105
    Is coming home today.

And it's buy a bunch of violets for the lady
    (*It's lilac-time in London; it's lilac-time in London!*)
Buy a bunch of violets for the lady;
    While the sky burns blue above: 110

On the other side of the street you'll find it shady
    (*It's lilac-time in London; it's lilac-time in London!*)
But buy a bunch of violets for the lady,
    And tell her she's your own true love.

There's a barrel-organ caroling across a golden street   115
    In the City as the sun sinks glittering and slow;
And the music's not immortal; but the world has made it sweet
And enriched it with the harmonies that make a song complete
In the deeper heavens of music where the night and morning
        meet,
    As it dies into the sunset glow;   120
And it pulses through the pleasures of the City and the pain
    That surround the singing organ like a large eternal light,
And they've given it a glory and a part to play again
    In the Symphony that rules the day and night.

                And there, as the music changes,   125
                    The song runs round again;
                Once more it turns and ranges
                    Through all its joy and pain:

97. *garland girls:* women who sell flowers.

233

Dissects the common carnival
    Of passions and regrets;   130
And the wheeling world remembers all
    The wheeling song forgets.

Once more *La Traviata* sighs
    Another sadder song:
Once more *Il Trovatore* cries   135
    A tale of deeper wrong;
Once more the knights to battle go
    With sword and shield and lance
Till once, once more, the shattered foe
    Has whirled into—a dance!   140

Come down to Kew in lilac-time, in lilac-time, in lilac-time;
    Come down to Kew in lilac-time (it isn't far from London!)
And you shall wander hand in hand with love in summer's won-
        derland;
    Come down to Kew in lilac-time (it isn't far from London!)

What is suggested by the different meters used in the poem?
Did the poet succeed in making you feel the spell of the music—
and of spring? Tell the class of some experience in which music cre-
ated in you a definite and deeply felt response.

ODE TO DUTY

William Wordsworth

For the last selection in our book of lyrics I have selected
Wordsworth's "Ode to Duty." This song is not played upon a barrel
organ, but upon the pipe organ in a magnificent cathedral.

Today it is popular to subordinate duty to other ideals: beauty,
happiness, self-expression, freedom. But, as Wordsworth so convinc-
ingly declares in this noble poem, all these are most fully attained in
the service of Duty.

This is great poetry. Give it the careful reading it deserves.

234

Stern Daughter of the Voice of God!
O Duty! if that name thou love
Who art a light to guide, a rod
To check the erring, and reprove;
Thou, who art victory and law   5
When empty terrors overawe;
From vain temptations dost set free;
And calm'st the weary strife of frail humanity!

There are who ask not if thine eye
Be on them; who, in love and truth,   10
Where no misgiving is, rely
Upon the genial sense of youth:
Glad hearts! without reproach or blot
Who do thy work, and know it not:
Oh! if through confidence misplaced   15
They fail, thy saving arms, dread Power! around them cast.

Serene will be our days and bright,
And happy will our nature be,
When love is an unerring light,
And joy its own security.   20
And they a blissful course may hold
Even now, who, not unwisely bold,
Live in the spirit of this creed;
Yet seek thy firm support, according to their need.

I, loving freedom, and untried;   25
No sport of every random gust,
Yet being to myself a guide,
Too blindly have reposed my trust:
And oft, when in my heart was heard
Thy timely mandate, I deferred   30
The task, in smoother walks to stray;
But thee I now would serve more strictly if I may.

Through no disturbance of my soul,
Or strong compunction in me wrought,
I supplicate for thy control;   35

But in the quietness of thought:
Me this unchartered freedom tires;
I feel the weight of chance-desires:
My hopes no more must change their name,
I long for a repose that ever is the same. 40

Stern Lawgiver! yet thou dost wear
The Godhead's most benignant grace;
Nor know we anything so fair
As is the smile upon thy face:
Flowers laugh before thee on their beds 45
And fragrance in thy footing treads;
Thou dost preserve the stars from wrong;
And the most ancient heavens, through thee, are fresh and strong.

To humbler functions, awful Power!
I call thee: I myself commend 50
Unto thy guidance from this hour;
Oh, let my weakness have an end!
Give unto me, made lowly wise,
The spirit of self-sacrifice;
The confidence of reason give; 55
And in the light of truth thy bondman let me live!

In the first stanza Wordsworth suggests that this "Stern daughter of the voice of God" might prefer some other name than Duty. What other name can you suggest for one who is "a light to guide, a rod to check the erring"? Explain the last two lines in the first stanza.

In stanzas 2 and 3 point out the lines that indicate the importance of duty.

Point out the lines in stanza 5 that show the superiority of duty over freedom.

Explain the meaning of stanza 6. Why does the poet speak of "humbler functions" in stanza 7?

Don't close this book without *feeling* the grandeur in the last two stanzas of this great lyric.

Index

Subject entries are set in roman type; title entries in italics; and author entries in capitals.

239

240

242